Still
STANDING
The Story of SSG John Kriesel

Still STANDING

The Story of SSG John Kriesel

by **JOHN KRIESEL** as told to **JIM KOSMO**

CONTENTS

CONTENTS

FOREWORD

The Rev. Dr. Martin Luther King said, "The ultimate measure of a man is not where he stands in moments of comfort and convenience, but where he stands at times of challenge and controversy."

We live in challenging times and ease and comfort don't build the world we live in. It takes hard work, guts, persistence and character. And it takes people who are willing to face adversity and overcome the odds.

Members of our United States military have stepped forward, raised their hands and said, "I will serve, send me." These amazing men and women are true heroes.

As elected officials, business and community leaders, and every day citizens, we owe all of our men and women who serve or have served in the United States military more than just our words of support. We owe them our actions. We owe them our deeds. And we owe them our eternal gratitude.

Staff Sergeant John Kriesel is an example of one of these amazing individuals. Like so many of his fellow soldiers, he served our country with duty, honor, courage, and incredible sacrifice.

On December 2, 2006, a roadside bomb tore through Staff Sergeant Kriesel's Humvee outside of Fallujah, Iraq, killing two of his best friends, shredding his body, and taking both of his legs.

and an outstretched hand that greeted every stranger with unbridled enthusiasm.

Do not extend pity, expect bitterness, or call John Kriesel a hero. He wears his bionic legs with extreme pride and delivers a message of hope for the world that he and the buddies he lost in Iraq firmly embraced. Heroes, he stiffens, are the guys who gave their lives and those who saved his life in Iraq, in Germany, and at Walter Reed Army Medical Center.

The guests at this fund-raiser were mainly business leaders, folks with money, power, and brains. Successful people. Strong, motivated, highly confident, inspirational people. So, it was with jaw-dropping astonishment that I watched the youngest person in the room, a guy who had already endured more hardship than all of us combined, raise every boat in our little pond to a higher level. At that moment something reached inside my head and screamed, "This guy has a story that must be told and you are the guy who must do it."

After the meeting, John and I paused at our cars to talk, ignoring a cruel twenty-mile-per-hour Minnesota wind and below-zero temperature. We met again a few weeks later at a restaurant in Woodbury and launched the book project. He kept thanking me for doing this for him and offered to buy breakfast.

"Obviously, there are times when it really sucks not being able to melt into the crowd, but I'm just happy to be alive. I realize I'm not normal any longer and I have a mission—I have learned many lessons that I must pass on."

That's what this book is all about, passing on the lessons learned by an amazingly positive young man who was driven to act when he recognized a threat to the American Dream. He paid an incredible price for what he believes and certainly has earned the respect of every American. His story definitely deserves to be heard.

In the process of scouring piles of data and interviewing many of Minnesota's "Red Bulls" for John's story, I made a series of discoveries—most important of which is that some things never change. I quickly learned that when you strip away the modern equipment, twenty-first century soldiers are no different than my brothers who fought in Vietnam; there is nothing particularly special about them other than *how they* performed under extreme circumstances. We're all brothers separated only by age.

These young soldiers are intelligent, caring people enriched with Midwestern values enabling them to withstand horrific challenges. In battle they understood and respected the Uniform Code of Military Justice; but more importantly, their strong family values guided their actions toward one another and the people they met, even the enemy. In war, compassion can be a dangerous companion, but it lives inside these soldiers. Bravo Company, a unit of nearly 150 soldiers, lost three and had five sent home with injuries. John was the unit's only VSI—very seriously injured.

These Minnesota National Guard troops clearly demonstrated what distinguishes the American warrior from insurgents. Their actions in combat proved what embedded journalist Karl Zinsmeister wrote for American Enterprise magazine, "The extreme care taken by U.S. forces to avoid civilian casualties in Iraq is in stark contrast to actions of the Fedayeen in Iraq who purposely involve innocent civilians in combat situations."

Living under the constant threat of death while isolated from friends, family, and every aspect of life as they had come to know it changed these soldiers. How these young people dealt with change is the important detail. Most of them came home and moved on to acquire college degrees and become valuable contributors to our nation as teachers, lawyers, bankers, police officers, medics, and more.

Some of these soldiers were damaged physically or mentally. Here again they benefitted greatly from strong programs, training, and experienced leadership in the military; but mostly, they recovered because of their solid foundation in American values and the deep, unwavering support of family.

One advantage of being in the National Guard as opposed to the active Army is that these guys came home together where they

Chapter 1

SURVIVING A
200-POUND BOMB

December 2, 2006

It's true, you really do relive your life as a high-speed video just before you die, and it's absolutely amazing how much you can remember in eleven minutes as you helplessly watch your blood stain the scorching sand in a growing pool of burgundy.

As my life pours into the desert in this God-forsaken Iraqi sand trap six thousand miles from home, I realize there isn't a damn thing I can do about it. Absolute paralysis grabs my body; hell, the lack of anything resembling legs and the sickening sight of my twisted, useless arm should toss me into shear panic, but it is the sudden fear that I am not going home, never going to see my beautiful wife, never squeeze my little boys again that is more painful than my massive wounds.

There's no such thing as a good day in Iraq, but today came as close to good as any day gets in this hell hole, until the left front wheel of our new, fully armored Humvee triggered a 200-pound IED (improvised explosive device). That damn bomb buried by some scumbag hajji wrecked a good day, igniting a hail storm of hot rocks.

It isn't panic, but a strange calmness that invades my senses, in all probability induced by a heavy dose of shock. I am awake, alert, and aware. That clarity of thought interrupts my life-story replay frequently with bursts of real-time action.

With great effort, I push up on my one slightly good arm and see that my left leg is severed just above the knee, attached only by a piece of skin with white, broken bone glaring back at me. I've never seen human bones before, especially not my own. The right leg looks more like fresh hamburger than a leg. God, my left arm is twisted into a pretzel; blood is running out of wounds around my mouth and, worst of all, my flack vest opened up during the blast, allowing my abdomen to take a serious hit. My right bicep is split open from shrapnel, and the bracelet I wore to honor a fallen soldier has sliced my wrist to the bone.

Pieces of the Humvee are scattered everywhere. All the doors are blown off; the right front door, a 400-pound piece of metal that takes three strong guys to lift, was tossed 400 feet like a Frisbee. This really happened to me, to us. I struggle to get out of the flak jacket, but it is impossible because my left arm obviously is broken in several places and the right one isn't much better.

Conscious of what is happening, I survey the pile of shredded metal that had been a sturdy battlewagon minutes ago; now it is difficult to recognize what it is. I stop, close my eyes, and pray. I know it's really bad, and I don't want to see any bodies that are ripped apart, that isn't going to be my last memory. I'm a trained EMT, and I can see as much as half of my blood already in the sand; that doesn't bode well for my chances.

Instantly, upon hearing the all too familiar, sickening sound of an IED blast SPC Adam Seed, driver of the lead vehicle—a heavily armed tank known as a M2A2 Bradley Infantry Fighting Vehicle— slams on the brakes. Turning back to look, Seed and the Bradley crew are engulfed in a sudden, blinding dust storm, but as the brown curtain settles, grim reality slowly emerges.

Cautiously, Seed rolls the Bradley back to the disaster scene, constantly surveying the ground for a second bomb, while watching the horizon for insurgent snipers. SGT Todd Everson relays the initial alert to Camp Fallujah, and SGT Adam Gallant focuses on the horizon from the machine gun turret atop the Bradley, aided by a high-tech scanning device with optics capable of zooming up to fifteen times magnification and a thermal imaging unit that recognizes objects that emit even the slightest heat signature from as far away as over 500 meters. The only limiting factor is that neither device can see through walls, doors, or very thick shrubs; but in an open environment, the thermal scanner lights up the outline of anything foreign, often objects that would not be expected to generate or hold heat. These high-tech devices, when combined with the keen eyes of a couple of guys like Everson and Gallant, who are as good as it gets, uncover dozens of IEDs every day. But even the very best are bound to miss one.

As Seed maneuvers alongside the shattered Humvee, shielding the south side of the blast site, Gallant and Everson vault from the Bradley and race to help. Gallant moves directly to the scene as Everson relays instructions to Seed, who remains on the radio while constantly scanning the area with the 25mm main gun ready to prevent further casualties.

"Call it in, Seed. Get a medevac chopper in the air fast," Everson shouts over his shoulder, relaying Gallant's plea as he races among the stricken Humvee crew.

They find the wreckage blown off the dirt road, flipped up on its side and facing the wrong direction. First they encounter SSG Tim "Nelly" Nelson who crawls out of the vehicle and drops in the sand twelve feet from the Humvee; he's suffering a back injury and concussion. Nelson is conscious but pretty incoherent as he sits there repeatedly asking no one in particular, "What time is it? What time is it? How are my guys?"

For some strange reason, I recall an incident a few months ago when Nelly and I talked about a guy who had lost a leg in an IED blast. I had told him, if that ever happened, to just let me die. Now that it has happened I just want to live. I hope he doesn't remember what I said. Is this my punishment for that stupid comment?

Everson and Gallant realize they need to tip the Humvee back down on what appears to be the bottom to get at SPC Bryan McDonough and SPC Corey Rystad, but first they pull me away and apply tourniquets to both legs. I was tossed free of the Humvee and planted in the sand with the shattered vehicle looming over me.

"This is going to suck," Everson says with pain in his throat as he flips what is left of my left leg up on my chest.

"Ahhhh," is all I can manage. There isn't any pain in my leg but the site of that mangled leg flopping on my chest is a clear message even a half-dead guy can comprehend, and the sting of injuries in my back and arms is more than enough. Lying in the desert I suddenly feel more like I'm buried in snow in the middle of a Minnesota winter, and I'm alert enough to realize that shock is sinking its fangs into my body.

Gallant returns. "Kries, I'm not going to lie to you. Your legs are really bad, but you're gonna make it, buddy. Just don't move and keep talking." Moving around the Humvee he spots LCpl. Bruce Miller who was blown roughly fifty feet from the gunner's hatch. Shaking his head clear, Miller gets to his feet and walks back to the blast site. Gallant determines that Miller's injuries are minor except that he is disoriented and may have a head injury.

"Everson, I need tourniquets," I speak up. In reality I already have tourniquets on both legs, but I'm not thinking or talking coherently. The one on my right leg is so loose it's not stopping the blood, largely because there isn't much leg to tie off on and the surge of blood is making it even worse.

"You got 'em, Kries," he assures me as he tightens the tourniquets. There is no medic with us today, but every infantryman is trained in basic battlefield first aid and, thankfully, Gallant and Everson were paying attention in those classes.

With Miller, Nelson, and me moved clear of the wreckage, Gallant and Everson instruct Seed to bring the Bradley closer to pull what's left of the Humvee back onto its base. Once the twisted steel drops back, they find SPC Bryan McDonough lying motionless, mortally injured. SPC Corey Rystad, who was partially under the vehicle is also severely injured but shows a glimmer of life. Gallant continues giving Rystad CPR while Everson re-wraps my legs with all the bandages he can find.

As we wait for the medics, Gallant and Everson move Miller and me further from the Humvee, claiming that they want us close to the helicopter when it lands, but I suspect they don't want us seeing McDonough and Rystad; and that's just fine with me. Everson stays with me and Miller while Gallant tends to Rystad and Nelson. Nelson tries to get up, but Gallant isn't going to let that happen. Rystad has stopped breathing, but Gallant continues to clear his airway and to force oxygen into his lungs. As long as there is any hope, Gallant is not going to give up.

Everson checks my tourniquets again and finds them falling off because of the bloody sheen cascading down both legs. Realizing the damage is so severe that legs are about to become irrelevant he cranks down on my tourniquets until blood loss stops and props what's left of my legs up on two MRE (meal ready to eat) boxes. Lunch definitely can wait.

"Tell Katie I love her," I implore Gallant.

"Don't worry, buddy; we got ya covered. You're gonna tell her yourself," he assures me with all the love and compassion every brother in combat has known since the beginning of time, bonded in the stark knowledge that "it could be me on the ground."

Everson orders Miller to sit beside me and keep talking. Miller goes on asking the same stupid questions and talking nonsense. Later I learn Everson just wanted to keep me conscious and alert, as alert as a guy with half his blood making mud in the sand can be. I guess he knew Miller needed the distraction, too.

Back at the Bradley, Seed is on the radio engaged in a shouting match with Bravo X-Ray, our tactical operations center. "Screw the ground ambulance, if you don't get a fucking medevac chopper here damn fast these guys are dead."

We are only four miles from Camp Fallujah where an Army ambulance has already been dispatched, but after the heated debate Seed wins the argument and a bird lifts off heading our way, ETA (estimated time of arrival) two minutes.

Gallant grabs a star cluster and waits for the bird to slide across the desert before slamming the bottom into the baked sand, deploying the red smoke grenade to reveal wind direction and our exact location for the chopper pilots, although it's not like there is a whole lot else to see on the barren landscape. With the bird on the ground, Seed bolts to the Humvee, loads Nelson on a flat board, and helps carry him aboard. The ground ambulance arrives almost simultaneously with the chopper, about eleven minutes after the blast.

Gallant hands off Rystad and Miller to the medics and approaches SSG Chadwick Lunsten, the QRF (Quick Response Force) commander, to advise him of casualties. Medics from the chopper give each of us a quick assessment before Gallant and Lunsten load me, Rystad, and Miller onto that big, screaming bird. Finally, Everson and a medic put McDonough into the ambulance.

Everson approaches the medics, stares in their eyes, points my direction, and shouts over the chopper's intense, rapping roar, "HE'S GONNA MAKE IT!" It's not a plea, prayer, or question, it's a fierce command, fired with more force than a four-star general could muster, and the medics respond with an assuring "yes, sir" nod.

For the first time, I have just the slightest glimmer of hope that I might actually survive.

Eight days later I cautiously ease open my eyes. Amid the blurred realization of consciousness I quickly wonder, is this heaven or something else? Then my personal angel comes into view, and it is my heaven with Katie at my side.

My injuries, though massive, are immaterial at the moment. I am just ecstatic to be alive. Moments later I discover I am at Walter Reed Army Medical Center in Washington, D.C., beginning a totally new battle that will test my courage and energy far more than anything Kosovo or Iraq has thrown my way.

Chapter 2

GROWING UP IN MINNESOTA

As a youngster growing up in Minnesota, I majored in mischief, constantly getting into trouble. I became a ridiculous smart-ass, ready to say anything anytime I thought I could get a laugh. Often I made some stupid comment in class, knowing it was going to get me sent into the hallway or down to the principal's office, but it didn't matter as long as I made the class laugh. It was fun.

I wasn't a bad student. Actually, in kindergarten I was the only one who could read; so, the teacher had me read to the other kids. My grades weren't very good, not because I was stupid as much as I just wasn't interested; although one year I made the honor roll, just to prove that I could. In hindsight, I see that I robbed myself, but I'm going to use my experience to make certain my kids don't make the same mistake.

Mostly I hung out with neighborhood kids, all of whom were three or four years older than I. I thought they were cool. Actually they were trouble, and they loved to use me to do their dirty work. I was always the one who got caught. We spent summers sleeping in tents so that we could play all night. We'd ring doorbells at two a.m. or TP someone's yard with rolls of toilet paper. At the time it really seemed funny. It was never anything serious; we just pissed off a few people. One guy came racing out of his house, jumped in a pickup truck and chased us all around the neighborhood. That was my first experience with urban warfare, and I loved the exhilarating charge it sent ripping through my chest.

In my sophomore year a boyhood dream of becoming a soldier surfaced, recalling when I was only nine in 1991 and the first Gulf War erupted as the world's first live broadcast war. I sat riveted to the action in the safety of our suburban home and I wanted to be a soldier. Now, seven years later I grab all the military brochures I can find and over the next few weeks visit military recruiters in every branch of the service. The Marine recruiter is an overzealous whacko; cross him off the list. I'm not much interested in flying over the action or watching it from a giant Navy yacht; so, that leaves the Army. I know I want to be boots on the ground, and the Army recruiter assures me, "That's what we do in the Army."

Army life is still more than a year away until I stumble onto an interesting opportunity with the National Guard—you need to be out of high school to join the active Army, but the National Guard offers a special plan where I can join at age seventeen and do Basic Training after my junior year in high school. The rest of the year I will attend weekend training and take my military specialty training after graduation. That sounds perfect and I can always transfer to the active Army later.

The Guard invites me to take a "first look" visit, a no obligation chance to check out Army life at Camp Ripley in northern Minnesota with other high school juniors. The first look is little more than that, a look. We make a quick tour of the base, eat lunch, and head home; but it's enough to convince me that I am headed in the right direction. It is very cool, very cool.

We go back to Camp Ripley for a "second look." This time it gets serious with real leaders, Sergeants Kane and Garza, who issue us camouflage uniforms, laser tag gear, and "real" M16 rifles with blanks equipped to fire laser light beams instead of bullets. The

Some people are
destined to be soldiers

In 11th grade just
before enlisting

equipment includes a special harness and helmet with a halo, nothing
angelic about it; but if you get shot by a laser beam, the helmet
beeps—no—it screeches.

Fully equipped and ready for war, we eagerly follow Kane
and Garza to scout out and attack a veteran infantry squad that is
hiding in the nearby woods. We never see it coming. They are well
hidden and quickly teach us rookies the difference between playing
soldier in our backyard tents and on the battlefield. We get blasted
with realistic-sounding ammunition, and for total impact they toss
simulated hand grenades that explode with the intensity of M80

firecrackers, almost delivering real pain.

The only way to stop the incessant, piercing beep from my halo is to remove a key from my harness that also disables the laser on my rifle—you can't shoot; you're dead.

It is truly a teaching moment; so, the proud tutors haul us back through the entire exercise, explaining with extreme pride each fatal mistake that we made and how to avoid doing that again when the bullets are real. I figure these guys mostly just want to demonstrate how lethal they are.

We all sit down and dine on field chow, fondly known as MREs, that seem quite cool—probably not so much after a few months on the battlefield. MREs are the much improved, modern equivalent of C-rations that were given to soldiers in World War II and the Korean War. Feeding men on the battlefield has always been a challenge, but time and experience has brought us a long way from the cans of mystery meat, salt pork, bread, coffee, sugar, and salt that comprised a day's rations in the Civil War.

Finally, our guides show us the tin huts where soldiers sleep six to a hut during training; well, not so much sleep as recharge. We witness an incredible display of professional-level beer drinking. Beer cans are stacked to the top of every window. The sergeant explains that his guys give their all during the day and then relax with equal intensity; maybe this training thing isn't so bad after all.

The next few months fly by, and it's October 7, 1998, my seventeenth birthday. No party, no gifts, no cake. I walk into the National Guard recruiting office in downtown Minneapolis with my buddy Chris Larsen, "that's Larsen spelled with an 'e.'" He adds the explanation so fast that it is practically part of his name. Minnesota is home to almost as many Norwegians and Swedes as is Scandinavia, and they wage their own ethnic war; but in this case they use Ole and Lena jokes and a disgusting, smelly, pale-white fish dinner called lutefisk for ammunition; that can get pretty painful.

Chris and I enlist and spend the day taking tests at the Minneapolis Military Entrance Processing Station (MEPS). They stick us in a hotel in the crappiest part of Minneapolis where we hear gunfire during the night and joke about being in our first battle zone.

I am already signed up for infantry, and that doesn't take a Rhodes scholar; so, I'm not worried about the test. My motto at the moment is: "work only as hard as you have to," but I know Chris will try his hardest no matter what.

The reading and writing portions of the test go smoothly as does basic math. The rest of the test is on a computer and going well until I realize the New York Yankees and San Diego Padres are playing in the World Series on television downstairs; I want to be down there. A dumb-ass seventeen-year-old, I just start pressing any keys on the computer to finish the test as quickly as possible. I score well, but I don't know if I just got lucky with the keys or did so well on the reading and writing portions that the computer section doesn't matter. I pass and shoot down to watch the Yankees smoke the Padres 9–3 to win the second game of the 1998 World Series. The Yankees sweep the Series four games to none.

Next morning we take physical exams, an all-day deal. We strip down to boxer shorts and parade through as they check range of motion in our arms, legs, and body. They inspect any tattoos to ensure that we have no gang symbols, offensive images, or anything that shows below our shirtsleeves. Next they look for any pre-existing conditions. Apparently some people try to use the Army solely for the medical benefits. Then we run the medical gauntlet with urinalysis, blood tests, allergy tests, height, weight, and all the rest.

That's it; the recruiters march us downstairs where we raise our right hands, say the oath, and officially sign in. You're in the Army now!

I am still half asleep from waking up so early, but for now, I just want to call home and tell Mom I made it. They don't want us using the phones in the Federal Building; so, I venture into the streets of downtown Minneapolis in search of a pay phone (cell phones were not in every pocket in 1998). The first place I come upon appears to be a restaurant; they must have a phone.

"How old are you?" asks some burly, no-neck dude in a dark suit designed for a smaller guy as he blocks my path into the restaurant. Without answering I quickly realize a "gentlemen's club" probably isn't the best place to make a call to Mom. I exit Rick's Cabaret and find a phone a few blocks away.

We go on the Army payroll, get assigned to the East St. Paul National Guard Armory, and start training one weekend a month. The very first real soldier I meet walking into the Armory is a short, stocky guy built like a diesel truck. The second my foot crosses the threshold he unloads a barrage of nasty comments and fierce instructions, barking, barking, barking.

Oh, Christ, what have I gotten myself into?

This, tiny mountain of muscle terrifies me, but it doesn't take long to realize he is a damn good soldier bent on giving us the best possible training. SSG Kelly Jones, a former Army ranger, is full-time director at the East St. Paul Armory, and there is no doubt who has the authority. He radiates an aura that says nobody messes with Sergeant Jones. If you are one of his guys, you know he's got your back; he'll do anything for you. Anytime another leader tries to mess with one of his guys they quickly feel the blazing wrath of Sergeant Jones.

Our first weekend drill is at the St. Paul Firefighter Training Center where we begin a course in urban warfare or military operations on urban terrain (MOUT) as the Army likes to call it. Essentially, it is war games without live ammunition, definitely more realistic and fun than paintball games. Once again we are issued laser guns and special uniforms that detect laser beams and emit loud screeches when you are hit, but the only real injury is to your pride; much worse is yet to come.

Weekends are spent at the Armory or Camp Ripley, a two-hour drive north from St. Paul, learning military codes and discipline, and mastering the proper clean and assemble techniques for our weapons. Repeatedly, the Uniform Code of Military Justice and

SSG Kelly Jones

Young recruit at basic training

Rules of Engagement are emphasized. The Code applies to every person in every branch of the U.S. military, and it prescribes exactly how a soldier must respond and conduct himself or herself when faced with various situations. The Code is constant, no changes or exceptions. The Rules of Engagement can change, depending on local conditions and level of threat, and go beyond The Code to describe precisely when, where, and how deadly force may be used in a specific area of operation (AO).

As training continues I realize that I like the Guard even more than I had anticipated. Suddenly I am with a bunch of guys just like me, and they are my life. Even when I'm not in training I spend my free time with them, usually with Joe Mehlhorn, an East St. Paul guy. Joe is not only a great friend, but he's the guy who brought Katie into my life. Joe met Katie and her friend Nicolle in seventh grade. He married Nicolle and introduced me to Katie, the love of my life.

Chapter 3

FORT BENNING

Summer arrives and it is time for some serious work: basic training at Fort Benning, Georgia. As a fired up seventeen-year-old kid, I walk purposefully through the Columbus, Georgia, airport and run smack into a gigantic floor to ceiling, deep-blue insignia bedecked with an enormous sword and the Fort Benning Infantry Training slogan "Follow Me."

"Wow! This is it!" I'm pumped.

My chest swells a few inches when a soldier dressed in perfectly pressed field greens approaches, greets me by name, welcomes me to Fort Benning, and leads me to a waiting Army van where I join a dozen other newbies. We see lights at the fort from the airport, but for some reason the trip takes almost an hour as we twist and turn through a maze of narrow roads without making much headway. Later I hear a rumor that new recruits always arrive at night and are driven around in circles for an hour to purposely disorient them and discourage the urge to go AWOL (absent without leave, over the hill). I don't know if that's true, but I'm discovering that anything is possible.

Once we finally land at the base, the driver drops us off at the

30th AG In-Processing Center where we fill out paperwork until our arms are ready to drop off. Our first day in basic training becomes a thirty-six-hour marathon of torture; well, not water-boarding or anything like that, but it sucks. We spend hours filling out mostly meaningless paperwork and sitting around waiting, a lot of waiting. At seventeen I'm used to getting plenty of sleep as most teens do; so, filling in the blanks on monotonous form after monotonous form is akin to dripping water on your forehead for hours. My eyes want to slam shut, but anytime one of us starts to droop some drill sergeant dumps a canteen of water on our head.

We stop for breakfast and stand in line for over an hour at parade rest, no moving, no talking, nothing, and keep your eyes straight ahead, private. We are all starving by the time we get something they call breakfast slopped into our mess kits. We jam the food into our mouths like a pack of rabid dogs. The mind games continue as the drill sergeant suddenly ends our feeding frenzy, bellowing at us to dump the remaining food in the garbage.

At long last, we get a few hours sleep, not nearly enough. Next stop is in-processing where we are divided into small groups and assigned to bays. Each bay has a name and we are the Night Fighters; at least it sounds pretty tough. The Night Fighters collapse into their bunks, lacking the energy to even talk. We no more than close our eyes and the drill sergeant whips open our door, bellowing louder than a foghorn. As bad as this is we're warned that it's nothing in comparison to what is yet to come "down range." Down range is what they call it when you actually get together with the full company and begin training. At this point we are all pretty intimidated, but still eager to get at it.

Anyone who has been through basic training knows exactly what happens next. It is pure hell just fighting the soupy, oppressive envelope of heat that grabs you the instant you fall out of your bunk before dawn, still half-asleep while the stifling, humid Georgia air squeezes your lungs more intensely with every breath. And, that is before we even start training.

There is one more stop before going down range. They haul us back to the In-Processing Center where we fill out more senseless paperwork, collect our equipment, get sized for uniforms and boots, and meet the Nazi nurse. It's difficult to tell if she was trained to be a brutal, blood-thirsty vampire or if that is just her natural character, but the padded room makes me think the brutality is part of the show. Padding apparently is needed to protect recruits in case anyone passes out or goes crazy at the sight of the super-sized hypodermic needles or the Nazi nurse as she proceeds to shout orders and enjoy inflicting pain a bit more than necessary.

"Left cheek!" she barks.

I decide to play with her a bit, drop my pants and turn the right cheek.

"Get to the end of the line and try again, stupid," she snarls.

I guess it isn't as funny as I thought. Eventually, I make my way back to the front of the line and this time I comply quickly and quietly with the left cheek. The Nazi nurse winds up and slams the needle into my ass just as hard as possible with a slight, sadistic smile sliding across her face. Not about to give her any satisfaction, I grin in mock defiance, pull up my drawers and move along. At least I didn't pass out like some of the other guys in the room.

Last stop is the dental check-up. Finally something goes smoothly and I head outside to sit, relax, and wait for our bus—we do a lot of waiting, fulfilling the time-honored military mantra, "Hurry up and wait." I pile my gear alongside everyone who survived the medicals and plop on the ground just as another crazy drill sergeant erupts on the scene.

"Kriesel!" he roars.

"Yes, Drill Sergeant," I snap to attention.

"You idiot, you failed to get your dental x-rays."

"Drill Sergeant, I did them."

"No, you did not. Get your ass back to dental and get your damn teeth x-rayed."

Obviously, there is no arguing with this nut. I grab my gear, race

Chapter 4

BACK TO TRAINING AT FORT BENNING

In 2000, while our classmates spend the summer after graduation partying, we head back to hell, aka Fort Benning, for infantry training. Sandwiching the final year of high school between basic training and military job specialty training is called "the split option." My buddy from East St. Paul Justin "Goose" Geslin from Circle Pines also does the split option. Heading to Fort Benning we meet up with two other guys, Andy Fraley, who I knew from basic training, and Mike Lathrop, a friend of Goose.

This trip to Minneapolis we get the VIP treatment at the Regal Hotel, a huge upgrade from the joint we had for enlistment. We are told to be in our rooms by ten p.m. and there will be bed checks. They also tell us infantry school will be like going to college and that the rough stuff from basic training is over. We are quite certain that's a lie; so, we decide to have some fun before shipping out to Fort Benning.

Goose magically makes a big bottle of vodka appear from his backpack. We party in the room; then, Goose dumps the remaining vodka in a water bottle and the four of us hit the streets of down-town Minneapolis. Being only eighteen we can't get into any bars, but Déjà Vu, a strip club, doesn't serve alcohol; therefore, customers only need to be eighteen. We enter, watch a couple of pretty hot ladies slide around the stage, and walk back to the hotel to crash.

Next day we endure a few more tests before heading off to Fort Benning, luckily a breathalyzer isn't part of the testing. At Benning we meet up with several of the guys who had gone through hell with us the previous summer. Amazingly, all four Minnesota guys, Goose, Fraley, Lathrop and me, end up in the same platoon; how cool is that? As we suspected, the first two weeks are a repeat of basic training while they make certain that everybody is in top fighting shape.

In the middle of the ten-week course, Goose and I are paired up for individual movement techniques (IMT) where we zigzag across a half-mile firing range, engaging targets while continuously moving forward. We start to feel like frogs constantly popping up and down as one guy jumps up and runs while the other covers him, firing at the enemy targets. Then the other guy pops up and runs. It's miser-ably hot; we've got a bulky uniform with equipment, and we take a bite of earth every time our chin slams into the baked, dry, clay soil, soil that offers the comfort of plywood and spits coarse sand into your uniform turning it to sandpaper, ripping your elbows bloody. It only takes fifteen minutes but it feels like hours. At the end we survey our bloody, bruised elbows and knees and exchange a vigorous high five for a job well done.

"What the hell was that?" the captain snorts in my ear as he grabs me from behind, lifting me by the chinstrap on my helmet, jerking my head around. "You did that IMT like a couple of pussies."

"Whatever," I spit out, pissed that he grabbed me. In my anger I fail to punctuate my comment with the mandatory "Sir." Goose's face instantly drains of color, and he grabs my arm, trying without success to stop me from opening my big mouth.

"Oh, you think that was good smartass? Well, then why don't

you two just show us all one more time how it's done."

Aw, shit, I should have remembered what happened with the Nazi nurse. I have always been a knucklehead, ready to say anything, anytime; and that tends to get me in trouble. I'm going to have to watch that, or at least be more careful who I offend.

Back at the barracks I take out my frustration on a clown who doesn't outrank me. This guy has a nasty habit of not showering after hiking all day, and he stinks like hell. It's gotten to the point where I can't sleep because of the stench.

"Geez, you stink. Take a shower," I rip him. "I can't stand bunking next to a slob."

"Mind your own damn business, Kriesel," he shoots back with a vicious glare. "I wash plenty."

"No, you don't."

That doesn't get anywhere; so, next day when he is out of the barracks I find a huge piece of tape and run it over his bed picking up hairs just like the sticky rollers used by fine ladies on their sweaters and dresses when getting ready for an evening on the town.

"Here's the evidence." I toss the hairy tape at him.

Everybody laughs and for the next week they pull hairs and dust bunnies from everywhere and pile them on his bunk. It is funny until a giant floor fan falls over and blows hair all over the barracks just before the drill sergeant arrives for daily inspection.

I score another memorable moment one morning while taking a leisurely shower when the drill sergeant arrives for bunk inspection. The drill is that everyone must immediately stand at attention next to their bunk. I grab a towel and assume the position. Unfortunately, I fail to secure the towel and as I snap to attention it falls to my feet; some of the guys are unable to avoid laughing.

"IS SOMETHING FUNNY, PRIVATE?" the sergeant bellows in Goose's face.

"Yes, Drill Sergeant! Kriesel, Drill Sergeant." It's important to toss in "Drill Sergeant" as often as possible. You can never say it too much, but just one omission can be disastrous. If it's an officer you and prepare for the final assembly before going home.

Throughout training everyone worked very hard with one exception, a guy who constantly kept forcing others to carry his gear in addition to their own. I don't feel that he deserves to be an infantryman. It really bothers me that he got a free pass when there are guys who were actually injured and didn't complain. Goose's feet are bloody, and he can hardly walk for three days, but he didn't stop once, we never knew he was in pain. He didn't even have a look of pain on his face.

With infantry training complete, we return to Minnesota to spend weekends at the Armory awaiting the call to help the Army in some international hot spot, but nothing comes. We constantly rehash the basics and then we're off to summer training at Camp Ripley. Now, we need to focus on specialized training as a weapons specialist or as crew member on a Bradley Fighting Vehicle.

I'm assigned to a Bradley Fighting Vehicle. On the Bradley team, you have guys who dismount with heavy weapons and attack on foot, boots on the ground, and that's what I want. What I get is being trained as a driver. The Bradley crew includes the driver, gunner, and commander; and in combat five or six infantry soldiers "boots on the ground guys" are loaded into the back. They dismount out the back ramp to patrol the area. As for the crew, we sit in the 32,000-pound rolling weapon, providing cover for the ground troops with our big guns.

In the summer of 2001, I'm at Ripley with Joe Mehlhorn, Goose Geslin, Eric Negron, and a bunch of guys from the St. Paul Armory. Our trip to Camp Ripley is a piece of cake this time around, no yelling or grueling marches, and we are able to head into Brainerd at night to drink. A few nights we don't get back to the barracks until about four a.m., and that makes the five-thirty a.m. wake-up call a tad rough.

For most guys turning twenty-one is the most important moment in their lives, until something actually significant happens. Being only twenty I decide, with strong encouragement from a barracks full of guys, not to wait another year. In reality bartenders rarely question soldiers about their age, but I am a bit worried because I have already endured the wrath of my first sergeant and company commander for altering the age on my military ID card, a serious offense in the military. I lost the altered ID card in the fall of 2000; unfortunately, it was found in St. Paul and returned to headquarters, causing me to be demoted from private first class to private (E-3 to E-1) for altering an official document. It was a stupid mistake, but I accepted responsibility and vowed never to do anything that dumb again. Unfortunately, I have no way of knowing that my squad leader, an unforgiving, by-the-book curmudgeon, is destined to be promoted and continue to punish me for the next four years.

In April 2003, the long-awaited call summons us to report immediately to the Armory. My heart is pounding as my head races through the options—Bosnia, Kosovo, Afghanistan, or Iraq; where do they need us?

"Okay, guys, listen up," Sergeant Jones barks. The Pentagon has issued a national security alert based on intelligence information hinting at the possibility of domestic terrorism in response to the pending invasion into Iraq, and we are ordered to protect the nuclear power plant in Red Wing.

"Red Wing? You gotta be kidding!" I slump back trying not to laugh or scream.

Well, at least it's something other than another damn training exercise, but guarding a power plant on an island in the Mississippi River thirty miles south of St. Paul isn't exactly the exotic assignment I anticipated. If nothing else, the defense of Red Wing proves to be a good opportunity to get to know SGT Jay Trombley, a former Army Ranger who left full-time service to become a St. Paul firefighter. I have never met anyone who loves his job as much as Trombley. Other than playing a wild game of Battleship, all he can talk about is being a firefighter. The first few hours, it's great. You need to find a lot of things to talk about just to stay awake in the middle of nowhere, staring into the woods for invisible invaders who

Infantry Division march into their home base at Fort Stewart, they are extremely proud of themselves and never fail to point out their Superman image for us lowly Guardsmen. More often than not they are pure assholes who consider us unworthy of being in their presence.

On weekends we occasionally get passes and head into Savannah. For Halloween we invade town and discover we are the only ones not dressed for the occasion, but life doesn't get much better than a few vans full of troops out to party. That is when I first truly realize what Army brotherhood is all about. In civilian life if someone gets sick or drunk or does something stupid, the others often find that inconvenient or something that interferes with their good time; and more often than not the "friend" is abandoned.

With soldiers, no one is ever left behind, no matter what. If someone drinks too much or gets sick, everybody sticks with him. If a guy is being an idiot, we get him under control and deal with it back at camp. If someone tries to start a fight with one of our brothers, no matter how it started, things just aren't going to work out well for that guy; because he is going to deal with all of us. You hear about people getting jumped, even famous sports "celebrities" like Denver Broncos football player Javon Walker getting robbed and beaten in Las Vegas, but that will never happen with a soldier—we stick together, no matter what.

We head home for Christmas, return to Georgia, and ship out to Germany, where the misery of living in a tent during the middle of winter is offset slightly by getting to see the sites and, best of all, tasting real German beer. Normally I'm a light beer guy, but there's something special about a good, dark German beer.

We are stuck in the mud, literally, two hours north of Munich, at Hohenfels Combat Maneuver Training Center (CMTC), part of the Seventh Army Training Command. The 40,000-acre training facility has been owned by the U.S. Army since 1951, providing realistic combat training for U.S. and NATO troops. When troops were ordered into Kosovo in 1999 the Army's 2nd Brigade, 1st

Armored Division created a little Kosovo at Hohenfels to provide advance training for as many as five thousand soldiers, with a wide range of combat scenarios.

Tucked into the mountainous Bavarian Alps area of northern Germany, Hohenfels is less than an hour drive from Nuremberg and the Czech Republic, and three hours from the Austrian Alps. When we manage to get leave, there isn't time for skiing the Alps; so, we opt for a beer hall in Munich where we quickly discover Germans don't like Americans. I always wanted to go to the Hofbrauhaus but it turns out they aren't very welcoming. "You can't come in here," the bouncer spits in broken English. One of our guys, Will Bernhjelm, was celebrating here earlier and slammed his glass a bit too hard, sending glass shards flying, annoying the guards; so, "No GIs." Okay, well we're certainly glad we helped you get rid of the Nazis and Communists.

Undaunted by rejection we head off to see one of Munich's famous nightclubs. "VIPs only," the dude at the door blurts. Four more places and four more "VIPs only" rejections. We start to wonder how a place like Munich can have that many VIP-only clubs until our German driver reveals that "VIPs are anybody but American GIs."

Mired in a mix of frustration and anger, we spot the New York, New York Gentlemen's Club that is pretty empty and, according to our driver, is welcoming to anybody with money, even Americans. We suck down a beer, decide not to donate any more American dollars to Munich merchants, and head back to the hotel where the bar is open all night. We play pool, drink, laugh, and have a great time.

In the daytime, Munich is a totally different place. People actually seem friendly as we walk the streets of a beautiful city that is so compact you don't need a car. We grab lunch at McDonald's for a touch of home cooking and a chance for me to dazzle the guys with my limited command of the German language.

Our stay in Germany is only a month of living in tents, but in the middle of winter slopping around in wet snow and ankle deep mud—a month is definitely long enough. For the first time I am wishing for colder weather and thinking that those winter training sessions at Camp Ripley were a cakewalk compared to slopping around and trying to sleep in this chilled quagmire. At least in Minnesota we know how to have real winter, a long cold season that keeps the snow firm and relatively dry, as opposed to Germany's frigid soup.

Chapter 6

HEADING OFF TO KOSOVO

Before we sink to the bottom of the giant German mash pit, training ends and we depart for Kosovo.

Our new home is a quintessential military outpost, a former Serbian artillery base located near Gnjilane, Kosovo, and it is pretty much a vacation spot; although our stay starts off a bit rough. Being a bunch of Minnesota infantry guys attached to the 1-113 Iowa Cavalry Squadron, along with some guys from Minnesota's 682nd Engineer Battalion, doesn't go well; maybe it's all those Iowa jokes Minnesotans love to tell coming back to haunt us. Do you know what the best thing to come out of Iowa is? Interstate 35 to Minnesota.

We are the attached group, so the Iowa guys feel superior and try to pass off all the shit duty on us. That doesn't sit well with CPT Tim Kevan, our commander, who storms into headquarters with steam flaring from his nostrils and firmly announces, "Hell no! My guys are not your slaves." That's the end of it.

Our job is "peacekeeper," which apparently means you walk around town smiling at the locals and sit in the coffee shops carefully massaging a cup of java for an hour or two while looking for anything out of the ordinary and keeping the Serbs and Albanians from killing each other—literally. While patrolling the streets of Kaminice, we talk with the people just as you would on the streets of St. Paul or Boston. Many speak English or we find a way to communicate. They are friendly in a restrained manner except for the kids who are just kids; they are totally open, exuberant, and fun. Kids are kids no matter where they live. If only we could eliminate the teens and young adults, and start over.

Goose and I get to know the kids of Kosovo

The place is almost like home to the point that I never feel we are in any serious danger in this miniature country of two million people, less than half the population of Minnesota. Roughly ninety percent of the population is Albanian with fewer than 100,000 Serbs remaining in areas protected by NATO after the 1999 war. Historically, ethnic conflict is huge, but the biggest problem definitely is unemployment. When NATO troops arrived, more than eighty percent of workers in Kosovo were unemployed. Our military presence and successful efforts at bringing the groups together has led to tremendous improvement, dropping unemployment to sixty percent. That's improvement but it's still worse than the Great Depression, a long way to go with plenty of fuel for anger remaining.

Nearly everyone endures some level of poverty and you can easily count the few who would even be considered on the low end of our middle class. Their biggest challenges are crime, smuggling, and the dirty deeds of desperate people who are forced to do anything to eke out an existence. In the bigger cities such as Pristina (Kosovo's capital city) there are more jobs, and conditions continue to improve slowly, thanks to our protection.

Patrolling the streets in Kosovo

The Serbian people actually appear to like Americans. The Albanian Muslims do not, but they respect our guns and they need us to hold back the flood of exiled Serbs from pouring back into Kosovo to exact revenge. In the rural areas, we discover good, hardworking, extremely poor folks who are more concerned with survival than politics, but the cities are filled with young people who seem generally worthless. Most of them just sit around in the coffee shops all day listening to American music. They love our culture, but they want everything given to them.

Camp Monteith, our home for the deployment, boasts a handful of concrete buildings but, mostly, it is a collection of semi-permanent barracks commonly known as South East Asia huts (SEAhuts) arranged in city grid fashion surrounded by guard towers, giant sand-filled HESCO barriers, and concertina wire. Since the end of the 1999 War, each KFOR (Kosovo Force) rotation has added improvements, making life just a bit better for themselves and those who follow. Monteith boasts a movie theater, café, twenty-four-hour chow hall, state-of-the-art fitness center, and a food court offering pizza, burgers, and just about everything an American tastebud might desire. The base is named for 1st Lt. Jimmie W. Monteith who received the Medal of Honor for heroism in the initial assault on the bloody coast of Normandy, France, in World War II.

On my first patrol, we go with the unit we are replacing and do left-seat, right-seat rides to get the feel for the job. Their driver makes the route and I watch; then I drive and he checks me out. My first mission is to establish a vehicle checkpoint, looking for anyone who might be suspicious or show up on the BOLO (be on lookout) list, a directory of people wanted for various crimes.

The first guy we stop hands me his driver's license, and the sergeant I am relieving demonstrates how to check it against the BOLO list. To our mutual astonishment the guy lights up the BOLO, a confirmed, direct hit.

Detaining my BOLO suspect

"Christ, I never actually had a hit," the sergeant says. We double- and triple-check the ID. It's a direct match on the bad guys' list. So, we arrest the guy and turn him over to the Kosovo police who are very excited to grab him. Like the sergeant before me, I never get another hit during my seven months in Kosovo.

We are in Kosovo as part of the NATO-led Kosovo Force peacekeeping effort, responding to massive violence growing out of the 1999 Kosovo Civil War. The war was relatively short, but the underlying mistrust and outright hatred between Albanians and Serbs lingers as strong as ever. That violence drove an estimated 150–250,000 Serbs across the Ibar River into Serbia and Montenegro, claiming that they continued to suffer persistent intimidation and harassment.

Back in Kamenice, Serbian Orthodox churches, shrines, schools, and cultural monuments were damaged or destroyed in blatant acts of Albanian vandalism. Our overwhelming military presence and intimidating weapons help maintain a fragile calm that seems to be holding, except for sporadic vandalism, until March 15, 2004, when an eighteen-year-old Serb, Jovica Ivic, is shot in a drive-by shooting in the village of Caglavica. Local Serbs flood into the streets in protest bringing traffic to a halt.

Just when it appears that cooler heads are gaining control, reports that three Albanian boys drowned in the Ibar River, near the city of Cabre, dump gasoline on the simmering coals of civil unrest. A fourth boy who survived the drowning claims they were chased into the river by Serbs with a vicious dog from a nearby village. Public appeals for calm disintegrate when Kosovo news media fan the flames of violence by broadcasting unconfirmed, sketchy details of the drowning, alleging the deaths resulted from Serbian attacks.

Within hours an estimated 51,000 people take to the streets in thirty-three Kosovo cities focusing anger on ethnic minorities, law enforcement officials, and NATO peacekeepers. Over the next two days, nineteen people die (eleven Albanians and eight Serbs) and a thousand are injured, including sixty-one NATO peacekeepers and fifty-five police officers. As many as 730 houses and thirty-six Orthodox churches, monasteries, and other religious and cultural sites are seriously damaged or destroyed, and 3,600 people, mostly Serbs, are made homeless.

Unaware of the riots, my squad is on routine patrol in a small village outside Kamenice doing a basic town search. In Kosovo it's easy to become distracted from the destruction and poverty amid the natural beauty of the majestic mountains and fertile, green rolling hills that surround the city. Just for an instant I am transplanted to southern Minnesota where the climate is similar and the serene pastures are nearly identical to Kosovo's lush farms nestled in the lowlands and scores of tiny streams slicing through the dark-green carpet spread at the foot of a mountain range that leaps to the sky. On close inspection the tranquil scenery is poisoned only slightly by piles of garbage strewn everywhere.

Everything is secure except for occasional signs of vandalism. Walking through the rubble I step on something, seriously sprain my ankle, and struggle back to the Humvee, barely able to walk. Standard protocol requires that an ambulance accompany us on town searches; so, I climb aboard to get my ankle examined and sit out the rest of the town search.

We're heading back to camp, barely out of town when the company commander orders the whole company to make an about face and set up a road block at the town's edge. While my platoon inches down the block through an incendiary crowd, I'm stuck in the damn ambulance. The mob begins to surge around us, screaming, chanting, and beating their fists and sticks on the ambulance. When they start rocking the Humvee, trying to tip us over, I've had enough.

Not about to become a victim, I grab my gear, cinch up my boot as tightly as possible, check my rifle, and climb out to greet the menacing mob. One guy charges forward, but I stop him in his tracks, slamming my rifle into his chest. As he falls back, the crowd suddenly realizes we have weapons and we mean business. They retreat rapidly.

A block away my platoon is in a shit-storm. With adrenalin as my crutch, I forget about the ankle injury and move down to help. We're vastly outnumbered, thirty-three soldiers against a mob of six hundred to eight hundred crazies, but our weapons more than balance the scale.

At first glance you might suspect the revelry is little more than a wild wedding party or soccer victory rally with all the car horns blaring, and drunks racing about. But flying rocks and Molotov cocktails tell us otherwise. As we push deeper into town, violence comes to a sudden halt—they learned long ago not to bring real weapons into any conflict with us if they plan to survive. Their primary weapons are their foul, loud mouths and a few rocks—no match for our rifles, riot grenades, riot gear, intimidating war wagons, and our attitude. We try Minnesota nice for a while. When that doesn't bear results we give them attitude, plenty of attitude. We have no clue what they are saying, but the tone of their voices and fire in their eyes needs no translation.

Our attention is drawn to an angry pile of protestors resembling a pulsating blanket of maggots swarming a dead carcass. Ever so cautiously we creep in that direction, pushing the crowd back to find out what they are devouring. Slowly they inch backward giving ground until an overturned yellow car smeared with blood emerges. The Serbian license plate reveals immediately that some poor soul is definitely in the wrong place at the wrong time.

"Man down, man down," somebody yells and we all think it's one of ours, but it's the guy from the car. Apparently he was just going to pick up his wife who works as a secretary at the local police station and, in the midst of the riot, he became chum in the water of protest for the Albanian radicals.

Victim's car after rescue, before it was destroyed by an arsonist

We spot the guy lying on the street badly beaten, bleeding profusely from a serious head wound. Jimmy Wosika employs some of his best Minnesota State Championship Wrestling moves to toss protestors out of his way, pulls the guy away from the crowd, gives first aid, and carries the guy to safety while the rest of us keep our guns trained on the angry mob that is salivating for an opportunity to finish off the hated Serb.

In the midst of the skirmish, Civil Affairs Officer Maj. Wilson shows up with his four-man team and asks to be attached to our platoon because he doesn't have sufficient manpower to deal with trouble alone. No problem. At that point it's organized chaos anyway with everyone melding in with the closest squad—Goose and I are stuck at one end of the street while Jimmy, Joe Mehlhorn, and the other guys in our platoon are down the street in Montero's squad. Once the victim is stabilized, Wosika and Joe load him into their Humvee and race off to the nearest hospital where the Serb is turned away in strong, clear Albanian words that translate into any language as "Go straight to hell."

Apparently the physician's creed hasn't arrived in Kosovo. They move on to the next hospital and get the same ugly message. I don't know how these people tell each other apart, but they do. Word of the incident races across town faster than Mehlhorn can drive.

Finally, Major Wilson calls a contact in Belgrade and makes arrangements for a Serbian ambulance to meet our guys at the Ibar River Bridge, Gate 1, for patient transfer. That works. Jimmy and Joe send the guy on his way thinking he won't survive the loss of blood and having his melon split open.

A few months later Wosika, Mehlhorn, Nielsen, and Wilson are reunited with the guy and his wife for a photo opportunity and story about their heroism in the local newspaper. However, Mehlhorn's Humvee never recovers from having blood sprayed inside as if from a lawn sprinkler. They strip out the seats and everything possible, but the putrid, metallic stench of dried blood never goes away.

Back in town the riot continues to sputter along, incited by one particularly angry guy. Montero keeps reminding everyone that battalion directive states if the crowd is more than ten people we're supposed to disperse them, but the lieutenant wants to negotiate. "Okay, you go with your plan," Montero says.

Smoke and tear gas cloud obscures angry mob as troops stand their ground

They approach the instigator, and the lieutenant tries to deal through Wild Man, our translator. The loudmouth isn't impressed or in any mood to negotiate as he demonstrates his English on the lieutenant.

"Fuck you," he shouts in nearly perfect diction.

The lieutenant struggles a few more times to talk peace, but every effort meets with the same obscene response and a single digit hand salute for emphasis—these guys are really catching on to American culture.

"Okay, Sergeant Montero, what do you suggest?" he concedes in frustration.

Montero turns to Wild Man. "Tell him he's got thirty seconds to make the crowd disperse or I'm gonna drop him."

The guy gives Montero the finger. Obviously, he's got enough talent to become a full-fledged American gangster.

"Tell him he's got fifteen seconds, now."

He flips off Montero again.

Montero loads a non-lethal sponge round into his shotgun, locks and loads, lifts the barrel and without further ado blasts the protestor in the chest, sending him tumbling, ass over teakettle.

There's no need to tell the crowd to disperse as they evacuate faster than rabbits spooked by a big dog. The guy is basically all right although he is going to be pretty sore for a while and his leadership abilities have just taken a major hit.

The next night we return to Gjilane where chaos erupts once more as the Albanians pour into the streets; they even let all their kids out of school early to join the fracas, flipping cars, setting fires, and threatening to destroy their own city. My squad spends the night stringing concertina wire to control the crowd, and our helicopters bomb them with tear gas.

By the third night we go back almost looking forward to the contest but nobody comes out to play. We're replaced by an engineering company, and they are flabbergasted by the fact that the locals are quiet, unlike what is going on in the rest of the country. One of the engineers asks, "What did you guys do to this crowd? It's like a ghost town." Almost as quickly as it started the riots are over and life goes back to what passes for normal.

My days in Kosovo brighten when the Minnesota Timberwolves climb into the NBA playoffs and suddenly I have something to talk about with the Albanians. Given the time difference, it's actually my nights that brighten, as I am up at three a.m. on game days to watch the games. Albanians are nuts about NBA basketball, although they absolutely hate Peja Stojakovic of the Sacramento Kings because he's Serbian. With Minnesota playing Sacramento, every Albanian is a Timberwolves fan. We celebrate the quarter final triumph even if none of them has the foggiest idea where or what Minnesota is.

A short time later Jimmy Wosika and I are resting on our bunks when the lieutenant calls and tells us to grab our gear and head to the helicopter for a mission to intercept smugglers. We exchange electric glances and leap to action, pumped with unbridled enthusiasm. Damn, some real action. Aboard the chopper we're briefed on the heinous crime of firewood smuggling. It's tough not erupting into laughter; but, strange as it sounds, smuggling wood is serious business in Kosovo. People get killed. There aren't many forest areas in Kosovo, but Serbia has vast forests. To be legal, firewood must be marked with an official stamp; so, we were constantly inspecting wood for the prized mark. Smuggling the precious firewood into

Montero, Kriesel, Yang and Wosika slosh through the mud searching for smugglers

Montero radios in our position

the country in itself isn't so serious; but, just as with the illicit drug trade, the primary concern is the gang-style activities it creates and how smuggling funds major criminal operations.

The chopper drops us off in the mountains where we watch for smugglers, laugh for three days, and talk about anything and nothing until our eyes cloud over—pretty similar to guarding the power plant in Minnesota. Man, we can't even get any action chasing firewood smugglers.

After seven months in Kosovo, we pack up and head home, feeling that our mere presence actually did some good for both sides; at least that's what CPT Kevan wants us to believe. There wasn't a lot of action, mostly because we were there; and while we spent our days talking to the Albanians on the street, our leaders were constantly bringing the Serbs and Albanians together in hope of reconciliation. Best of all, we all come home safely.

The only real downside is that my platoon sergeant apparently hates my guts and refuses to give me any opportunity to succeed. As an E-4 I'm automatically on the promotion list, but everything is based on points earned in the eyes of my platoon sergeant. I actually lost points in Kosovo, which makes no sense when you consider that I received several awards during the deployment. The only rationale he offers is that stinking drinking incident four years ago when I was twenty and altered my ID.

Unfortunately, in the military you are stuck with your leaders no matter what, and that is driving me crazy. My contract with the National Guard is about to expire; so, as we head back to Fort McCoy, Wisconsin, I decide it's time to go back to my civilian job at the ink factory. My by-the-book curmudgeon platoon sergeant has crushed my love affair with the Army. I want out.

Chapter 7

LURED BACK TO THE ARMY

January 2005

Home from Kosovo for three months and I'm still wrestling with the decision to stay in the Guard as my enlistment is about to run out. Finally, I convinced myself that it's time for a change, but before my new life plan takes shape my future threatens to take a U-turn when SFC Casey Courneya, a guy that I knew from my time in the 2–136th Infantry Battalion, calls out of the blue. Courneya and SFC Rene Montero, two guys I truly respect, are working at the Guard's brigade headquarters unit in Stillwater, and they want me to stay in.

"Tell me you're not getting out," Courneya starts. "Dammit, Kriesel, you just need a change of scenery." He goes off on me for five minutes until I begin to wonder, *Do you still call it a conversation if only one person talks?*

"I've had enough," I finally squeeze into the one-sided discussion. "I've been in the Guard for six years, watched all of my friends get promoted, and my platoon sergeant won't give me a break."

"Okay, Kriesel, what about Iraq with a different unit?"

"For real?" The possibility of going to Iraq and actually making a difference in the world turns my new plan upside down.

"Real as it gets, buddy."

Now, what do I tell Katie?

Armed with new information from Courneya, I realize that I really miss being a soldier and now there is a way to go to war with a unit composed of guys from East St. Paul and Alexandria. My challenge is telling Katie. I fear that more than anything. She isn't going to like this one bit.

We sit down to talk, and somehow she knows what's coming before I move my lips, and she's not going to make it easy. Obviously, it isn't what she wants to hear. She doesn't get angry, and that is almost worse.

Calmly she explains that she knows the military is a major part of who I am. She adds that she won't give me an answer because if she says "yes," and something happens to me, she will feel responsible, but at the same time, she can't say "no" to something she knows I believe in so strongly. Finally, she says she doesn't want me to have any regrets later, tells me to follow my heart, and vows that she will support whatever I decide. *Great*, it's my decision. She should be a politician.

After a long pause, I turn to her and plead, "Katie, you need to promise me that if anything happens to me you won't go on television and criticize the war; don't go Cindy Sheehan on me (mother of a fallen soldier who protested for months outside President Bush's ranch in Texas). And, don't let my boots be used in one of those anti-war demonstrations."

"JOHN!" she shoots back in an uncharacteristically firm response. "Both of my grandfathers fought in World War II and my brother is in the Army," her laser eyes slice through me with a look that is more disappointment than anger.

Her mother's father, David Beccue, fought off hypothermia, fatigue, and fear, floundering in the ocean for three days after the USS Helena was torpedoed near Pearl Harbor in 1941. "The Army is part of who you are; it is part of why I love you," she looks into my heart.

Some battles are not worth fighting, and I am definitely getting in over my head on this one. I smile, give her a long kiss, and drop the issue.

The only complication comes when I realize Army regulations prevent anyone from being redeployed to a combat zone within twelve months, and I have been back from Kosovo for less than a year. At this point, if I elect to go, I need to sign a waiver.

I decide to talk it over with SSG Kelly Jones, my old boss at East St. Paul Armory. He knows more than most entire platoons, and he's pleased that I am considering Iraq. He encourages me to follow my heart. Great, somebody else tossing the decision back in my lap.

They got me. The more I think about it, the more I realize I miss my guys, I miss the Army, and I miss the action and the discipline. Courneya and Montero pull me into Headquarters Squadron in Stillwater, but aside from a couple guys at the top of the food chain, I don't know a soul in Stillwater. Part of my re-enlistment deal is that I will have a good chance at getting into the Primary Leadership Development Course (PLDC), but first I need to complete a Combat Lifesaver Course. Stillwater has already completed the course, but good fortune smiles on me when I discover that East St. Paul has a course about to start and I can return to my old unit, if only for a short time.

Combat Lifesaving is going smoothly when another voice from the past pops into my ear. Jay Trombley, one of the squad leaders in Kosovo and my partner for the defense of the Red Wing nuclear power plant, is back with the St. Paul Fire Department. He calls to tell me the Department is hiring and that tryouts will be held in the spring. "Stay in shape; you're a perfect candidate for the Fire Department," he encourages. "Get certified as an EMT."

In Kosovo, Trombley became one of my best friends. Just like when we guarded the power plant in Minnesota, he was constantly talking about the St. Paul Fire Department; so, it's no surprise that he is trying to lure me into the job. He explains that being a fireman is not so different from being a soldier—you have uniforms, obey a chain of command, undergo constant training, and save lives and property; but normally you don't need a bulletproof vest.

Hovering over everything that I think and do is the shadow of Iraq. We hear that deployments are coming down within a year. No one knows for sure, but Iraq is a big part of why I re-enlisted. Until we get the call, the Guard is a part-time deal, and my family needs a full-time income. So, I return to my job at an ink factory, pumping colorful liquids into giant cans for the printing industry. It's an exacting task demanding precise adjustments and testing to ensure that ink colors are produced according to exact standards. Long term, the Fire Department still looks good.

Trombley works out of St. Paul Fire Station #17 at Maryland and Payne avenues, only a few blocks from the East St. Paul National Guard Armory where we train. After talking with me, he realizes everybody in our unit is doing Lifesaving Training, a requirement to be a firefighter, and he convinces CPT Stan Lewinski that the Guard offers a prime pool of hot prospects for the fire department. They quickly load up a fire truck and roll down Maryland Avenue to the Armory where they hand out thirty job applications to me and my buddies Jimmy Wosika, Mike Petschel, and Scott Sherwood.

With the lifesaving course complete, I head out to Stillwater for Guard duty. It's tough not knowing anyone and even worse once I get to know them. Right from the start I see that this unit doesn't compare to East St. Paul. These guys really are weekend soldiers who don't take anything seriously. They have strong leaders who must be about to go crazy with these guys. I struggle through until April, but don't feel any camaraderie with this bunch.

Keeping my options open, I continue to pursue a job with the Fire Department. Applying to be a St. Paul firefighter is the easy part; getting through the physical skills challenges, written exams, and personal interviews is downright daunting. But my chances dim under the weight of the Equal Opportunity Act that makes the path to success extremely steep for white males by giving women and minority candidates a significant advantage.

Before I know which direction I'm headed, my orders for PLDC come down and I'm off to Fort Lewis, Washington, for leadership training and a good shot at being promoted to sergeant in the National Guard. At graduation I am named to the Commandant's List, an achievement of extreme pride. In fact, for just a moment I want to call my old platoon sergeant to share the good news, but quickly move on to more positive thoughts. If nothing else, perhaps I should thank him for being an inspiration.

During the two weeks at Fort Lewis, I discover that old sense of service again and realize I have to find a way out of Brigade Headquarters. It's a pack of clerks and office guys who have a job to do, but it isn't the job I want. I'm a boots on the ground combat guy. As if to drive the point home, we're going through drills at the Stillwater Armory and one meathead POG (person other than a grunt) utters, "I don't know why we're learning all this crap. We're not going to be the ones being blown up. We're going to be listening to that shit on the radio." I want to drop that idiot right in his tracks. The "ones being blown up" he's talking about are my brothers in East St. Paul, and it makes me crazy.

I call Jones, explain my dilemma, and tell him I would rather go to war with Alpha Company as a driver or gunner and the rank of specialist than be at Brigade Headquarters with a bunch of desk jockeys. He promises to do what he can.

Uncertain about what will happen with the Army, I sign up for the Emergency Medical Technician (EMT) course at Inver Hills Community College, and I continue my pursuit of a job with the fire department, in spite of the "un-Equal" Opportunity Act complications. The EMT course begins in June 2005, and school is going great for me now that I am doing something that I love. For some hands-on training, I spend a night in the emergency room at St. Paul Regions Hospital. On arrival I discover the ER is short-handed so my observation session becomes a bit more hands-on training than anticipated.

A motorcycle accident victim arrives, suffering severe head trauma, and I watch as the ER staff battles ferociously to save his life, to no avail. After he is pronounced dead, I help clean him up before his family comes to say good-bye, but nobody comes. We slide him into a body bag and then into the cold drawer in the morgue as casually as you put away the silverware after washing your holiday dishes. I say a quick prayer for this guy; it just seems that somebody should acknowledge his life.

Our next patient is an elderly woman whose heart has stopped beating. The ER tech does chest compressions to keep her heart pumping until he's exhausted. I'm shocked when he waves me in. I thought I would be watching the action, not actually doing anything; but I am CPR trained. Sadly, that isn't enough. So far, this is a pretty depressing adventure.

Despite the two very sad stories, the night eventually yields some positive experience. People who have been in serious accidents, most with broken bones, arrive and are treated successfully. Some of the people with relatively minor injuries actually say, "Thank you." It's a fantastic feeling helping people, and I realize this is for me; I want to be a paramedic and plan to continue my education after Iraq to make it happen.

Chapter 8

GETTING READY FOR IRAQ

July 2005

I'm having lunch at Chili's in Maplewood with my friend Matt Tauriainen from Green Bay when Sergeant Jones calls. "I ripped up your papers," Jones says. "They are shifting a lot of people around for deployment to Iraq, and you are going to be with some guys you don't know in Bravo Company."

Hell, I don't really know the guys I'm with now; how can this be any worse?

Jones says I will have a good chance at becoming team leader with a very good shot at making sergeant and be assigned to Bravo Company, 2nd Battalion of the 136th Infantry from Crookston, a small town in northwestern Minnesota. That seals the deal; I'm going to war. Okay, there are a few stops along the way before marching into Iraq, but I'm on my way.

I'm flying high with the news, but when I tell Matt he gets very serious and says he's worried. Knowing how much I want this, he reluctantly claims to be happy for me, but he doesn't look happy.

I break the news to Katie. She knew it was coming and was

prepared, but confirmation is sobering. The rest of the summer I go about tying up loose ends and spending every possible minute with Katie and our sons, Elijah and Broden. Knowing the dangers ahead I do a lot of things that I always wanted to try; I want no regrets.

Summer is winding down without word on deployment; so, I take the EMT National Certification Test and then decide to hit Las Vegas for some serious entertainment. I love Vegas but my mind is riveted to the computer, constantly checking for test results. Finally, late the second night, up pops the test posting and there I am, a certified EMT-B on the National Registry. Tempering my excitement slightly are the wall-to-wall news reports of the savage attack by Hurricane Katrina on New Orleans, Louisiana.

Returning home I quickly discover getting certified as an EMT is only step one. Getting a job requires an opening in the fire department, and nothing is available. Trombley invites me to come on a ride-along shift at Station 17. Firemen love bringing in ride-alongs he tells me because it's just like taking an umbrella to the ballgame, insurance that guarantees nothing will happen. Nothing does, absolutely nothing. But Trombley pulls out a primitive Texas Hold 'em game that works with the firehouse television set, and we spend most of the twenty-four-hour shift throwing down a vicious battle of poker, feeding my growing passion for the game.

Before a job opens up with the fire department, it's mid-September and the National Guard finally calls. My buddy from Alpha Company, Joe Mehlhorn, and I carpool to Camp Ripley for a two-day Soldier Readiness Station where we get briefings on what to expect and what is expected of us. They check our records to ensure that we are fully deployable. This is the point where the Guard pulls aside the slackers who can't or won't cut the rigors of real military service. A few of them, who joined the Guard just for the benefits, figuring they would never have to do anything more than march in a parade, go camping, or stand guard at a flood, show up with a laundry list of excuses.

Now, I have an even tougher task, explaining it to my sons. Elijah is four and Broden is three. This calls for a special family vacation. We go for a week of splashes at an indoor water park in Brainerd. Family time is fantastic, but talking to the boys isn't any easier than it would have been at home as I carefully explain that I am going far, far away to a place called Iraq to fight the bad guys so that everyone there can be free to live like us.

"Are you going to die?" Elijah goes right to the point.

"No, absolutely not," I assure them.

"Are you going to come back okay?"

"Yes, I'll be fine."

They give me a couple of those uncertain smiles, and we go back to having a good time.

There was a day when criminals and cowards were pushed through for deployment, but those days are gone. Today's professional Army is only for highly qualified, committed, and skilled volunteers. For a moment I question that philosophy and then ask myself, *who do I really want my life to depend on in battle?* Unfortunately, there also are some very good guys who are pulled out for medical reasons, something as simple as an allergy to bee stings may prevent a soldier from deploying to battle.

We are given a little time off and told to report to the Alexandria National Guard Armory, one hundred miles northwest of Minneapolis, in two weeks for the flight to Mississippi before heading off to Iraq. It's a last-minute briefing and readiness session, but mostly a check to ensure that no one has gone AWOL. I hustle home to spend as much time as possible with Katie, Elijah, and Broden.

Reality of separation really starts to sink its claws in a week later and it hurts so much I can hardly think on the drive to Alexandria. This is unquestionably the toughest day of my life. As badly as I want this assignment, the reality of leaving Katie and the boys six thousand miles behind is pure torture.

In "Alex," one of the nation's great fishing holes, we don't get to do any fishing but Katie and the boys join me for two nights at the hotel. The third night it's just soldiers before we travel to the Moorhead

National Guard Armory to join with the entire 2–136th Infantry Battalion.

At long last I get to meet the guys of Bravo Company who will be going to war with me. The majority of them are the way-up-north, Iron Range types from some of Minnesota's tiny villages that have total populations smaller than my high school. Maybe being born in Hibbing somehow helps me fit in with the farm boys, even if I only lived there until I was two. Could it be genetic? We barely have time to pick up our gear before we are loaded onto a Northwest Airlines charter flight to Keesler Air Force Base near Biloxi, Mississippi, where we pile into buses and drive an hour north to Camp Shelby. They haul us right past all of the barracks on base out to a mock battle area where training is underway the second we step off the bus. It's dubbed Forward Operating Base (FOB) Hurricane, a clever reference to nature's recent assault on the area by Hurricane Katrina.

FOB Hurricane is set up as much like Iraq as possible for a realistic training exercise; Katrina helped prepare the faux Iraq site by clearing the area of trees and vegetation. It gets intense immediately as we set up guard stations and establish foot patrols around camp. Housing is tents, with the biggest one serving as chow hall. My new boss is SSG Tim Nelson, and he looks to be about a junior in high school. My first impression is shock at how young this guy is compared to the squad leaders in East St. Paul. As with everything in the Army, first impressions are always wrong. Nelson previously was on active duty with the 3rd U.S. Infantry (Old Guard) in Washington, D.C., where he served as a member of the elite "Escorts to the President" and was called into action at the Pentagon moments after the September 11 terrorist attack.

He looks younger than he is, probably his Scandinavian genes, but the guy quickly demonstrates that he is a solid soldier with plenty of experience and knowledge. Being six-foot-three and over two hundred pounds of muscle also helps overcome any concerns.

I look over the list of my guys without seeing anyone I recognize, but one name stands out, Corey Rystad. I don't know him, but one of my buddies from Fort Stewart and Kosovo was Dave Rystad, and I'm thinking there can't be that many Rystads in Red Lake Falls. Once we get to Camp Shelby, Corey confirms that Dave is his brother. A short time later, the brothers are talking by phone and Corey hands it to me.

"Hey, Kriesel, what's up, man? Corey's a great kid. Take care of him for me, and bring him home safe."

"You got it, buddy," I assure Dave. (Little do I know just how wrong I am. There's no way to describe the pain of losing a great friend and then having to tell his brother, mother, and dad that you couldn't keep him safe. War is shit and I don't care what you believe; it will test your faith over and over and over. There is no justice, no sense, no safety. It's just war.)

The rest of our time is focused on general readiness training and plenty of classes on warfare, Code of Conduct, and weapons training. One Sunday we're at the firing range, waiting for our turn to enter the range, and I'm going nuts wondering what's happening between the Vikings and Bears, when I get a brilliant idea. I call Katie's cell phone and ask her to lay it next to the radio for the game. This works great as I turn radio announcer shouting out plays between machine gun reports, except that the station Katie has on fades out every now and then and I can't call her to complain because her phone is already in use. Worse than the static, the Bears pummel the Vikings 28–3.

When we finally get on the range, the shooting goes well; maybe it's just a good chance to vent our frustration from the game on those dark, shadowy figures popping up as targets. A serious problem at Camp Shelby is the lack of firing range space for the number of troops. It's a major problem for us because we need as much training time as possible to prepare for combat, but everybody needs to qualify on the range no matter what job they have.

After a trip home for Christmas, we head back to Camp Shelby for final preparations to enter "the box" at Fort Polk. It's a six-hour ride to Fort Polk, Louisiana, where we spend another two weeks getting our gear ready before actually going "into the box," a mock battle zone complete with Forward Operating Bases and simulated Iraqi villages designed to be just like where we will live in Iraq, with frequent simulated mortar attacks. We're constantly on guard for insurgents played by a unit named Geronimo comprised of active duty guys, including a few who served in Iraq; they have been there and they know what's coming for us.

Finally it ends; we head back to Camp Shelby and get a break before heading off for the real thing. The final ceremony is set where guests and families are invited to sit in viewing stands just like at a high school football game as the entire Brigade, some 3,800 soldiers, emerges from the woods, marching in full battle gear. It's pretty impressive even for us, and Katie says it rippled her arms with goose bumps, although the pouring rain may have had as much to do with her chill as anything. As we pass in review Minnesota Governor Tim Pawlenty, Lt. Gen. Raymond Odierno, and Maj. Gen. Larry Shellito are among the dignitaries standing out in the rain, saluting.

Before heading off on a four-day pass, we need to turn in our weapons, and that can be quite the process. I just want to see Katie and the boys and get on the road; so, I run as fast as possible to turn in my weapon. I actually beat everybody, clear quickly, change into civilian clothes, and head off.

Katie pulls out the map we had been given earlier along with a stern warning not to go outside the big red circle drawn on it. Using the map, we had made reservations in Pensacola inasmuch as the 'P' in Pensacola is just inside the circle. What we don't have is the time or options to deal with two dripping-wet kids; so, we strip them down to their undies, cover them with blankets, and strap them into their car seats. They look so cute and funny at the same time that I can hardly stop checking in the rearview mirror and laughing. Always the show dogs, they are quick to grab the idea and start performing, even after one hundred miles their antics are still cute.

In Pensacola Beach we grab a room and head for the beach where we encounter a few other soldiers, including my guys, Bryan McDonough, Jimmy Wosika, Corey Rystad, Josh Hatton, and Brian "Boot Camp"

Micheletti. It's a beach party with little Brody and Elijah, the only kids, hamming it up for the crowd. Rystad gets into the act, letting the boys bury him in the sand while everyone laughs hysterically. The boys have never seen the ocean before; so, I grab a little paw in each hand and step into the oncoming waves. Elijah doesn't want any part of that and runs back to play in the sand. Brody can't get enough of the wave action. He loves getting tossed head over heels every time the tide blasts him. He could go on forever. Back on the beach, he grabs Katie's hand and tries to drag her into the sea, "Again, again."

It's amazing how fast four days can evaporate when you're having fun, but we head back and manage somehow to say our good-byes, knowing that this is going to be a long separation with real danger ahead. Still buried in a cloud of anxiety over their departure, I stumble into the battalion's barracks. At first it appears that a 500-pound bomb was detonated blowing mattresses and debris everywhere. There are bodies scattered across the floor, but before full panic sets in Luc Moua lifts his head and groans weakly. He's limp, lying on his mattress on the floor next to his bed. It turns out his buddies pulled him down from the top bunk to save him from falling in the night. These guys are bombed, but it wasn't enemy action, just one hell of a wild party—what did I miss?

Before heading out, it's time to clean the barracks, a task I decide to leave largely to the party boys, as Everson and I grab our gear and head out for a pizza while he fills me in on the gory details of the all-night celebration.

Chapter 9

TOUCHING DOWN IN THE THEATER OF BATTLE

Before arriving In Iraq we land in Buehring, Kuwait, where we pull our ID cards through the machine just like swiping a credit card at the Target store cash register, except we are checking in and the computer is officially logging the exact moment that we arrived in the theater of battle.

It's March 27, 2006, and we spend the next nine days waiting, training, waiting, and waiting some more, alongside fifteen thousand other soldiers in a dust bowl where about the only other living things we see are the infamous dung beetles, an incredibly ugly insect the size of a rodent. This creepy, oversized June bug is nature's sanitation system, devouring massive piles of dung, scat, shit, crap, or waste, whatever you want to call it. There is plenty of it in the nearby desert, dropped by roaming goats, sheep, coyotes, and camels--lots of camels, more camels roaming around the Middle East than squirrels in Minnesota, and they keep the dung beetles busy. Why do we have so many names for shit? And, why would anything eat it?

Even the slightest breeze lifts a wall of the brown powder off the ground quickly coating everything in sight, if sight is even possible. Walking to the Post Exchange, I feel my way like a blind man; my mind drifts home to a ride on an all-terrain vehicle through a sand pit last fall in northern Minnesota where I was eating dust from my family. That was actually gritty, real sand. This crap is so fine it filters through the walls of your tent, coats your eyeballs, and fills your ears. It's so damn miserable.

If you ignore the fact that every breath coats your lungs with brown dust, Camp Buehring isn't half-bad; although, it feels like something out of a *Star Wars* movie as I stumble through the brown fog and discover two Subway stores, Taco Bell, Burger King, Panda Express, a coffee shop, and a general store (the PX).

We're told to be ready at all times to ship out on two-hours notice, but as the days pass we wonder if it will ever happen. Let's get on with this damn war and go home.

Army life is proving helpful to my poker skills, and I use my personal time to refine those skills, reading everything I can find, watching videos, and practicing to the point where I have become a pretty good card player; so, I jump into a serious Texas Hold 'em tournament with thirty players at the MWR (a place officially labeled by some Army PR guy as the Morale, Welfare, and Recreation Center). Things are really going my way, as we drop under twenty players and my pile of chips towers over all the others, when Jimmy Wosika slides next to me and whispers that we just got notice; it's time to go to war.

Damn. I wait for my next hand, throw down "all in" with my worst hand of the night, and walk away a loser. God, I hate doing that.

Buses and a trailer truck arrive at the staging area near our tent at 0145 hours. We load our duffel bags and rucksacks onto the truck, manifest, and board the buses. Manifesting is taking roll call to ensure that everyone is accounted for before boarding the bus. Once manifested we ride out to a heavily guarded little air base in the middle of nowhere that they call "Area 51" where we sit and wait, as usual, until 0800.

I grab some sleep inside the waiting tent before we pile on a bus and head out to a C-130 Hercules cargo plane for the hour-and-a-half flight to Al-Taqaddum Air Base (affectionately known as TQ), a U.S. Marine base forty-six miles west of Baghdad at Habbaniyah. In the air it suddenly strikes me just how crazy things are about to get. Every other time that I've flown in a C-130, I've worn a soft baseball cap and headphones, and just relaxed or read. This time I'm wearing my IBA (interceptor body armor), Kevlar, an M4 carbine rifle, and 210 rounds of live ammo. This time I am flying into a combat zone.

Military body armor is constantly under scrutiny and debate; how do you provide maximum protection without hindering mobility? Designers are constantly searching for new ways to improve Freedom of movement and to reduce the weight of body armor without compromising the ability to stop bullets and shrapnel. The Interceptor Multi-Threat Body Armor System consists of an outer vest made of Kevlar weave capable of stopping a nine mm bullet, with small pockets for inserting SAPI plates placed strategically to protect vital organs, with optional throat and groin protection. The small arms protective inserts (SAPI) are made of boron carbide ceramic material with a spectra shield backing that is incredibly hard. The Army says SAPIs will stop bullets and fragments up to a 7.62 mm round with a muzzle velocity of 2,750 feet per second. Hopefully that's good enough. The IBA package weighs approximately thirty-three pounds.

Giant ninja turtles best describes the look we assume with our IBA system, and that's pretty much how it works. Just like a turtle, our massive protective shell shields the main part of our body and vital organs from bullets and most explosions, but not our arms and legs.

Heading into a real battle zone also changes the way the plane operates. Instead of flying in its normal point A to point B mode as the plane approaches TQ, the pilot suddenly executes a series of sharp, seemingly erratic maneuvers, banking and dropping, tossing us back and forth in a precautionary procedure to avoid the potential dangers from insurgent anti-aircraft fire. Without advance notice we slam into the ground harder than I have ever landed. The plane bounces twice, the pilot slams on the brakes, emulating a race car at the end of the track, and we are jerked forward, testing the strength of our seatbelts just like those test dummies you see in car commercials. The high-speed, controlled crash landing is required to avoid attack, and it is far more energizing than any carnival thrill ride and definitely better than getting blasted out of the sky. A couple of guys lose their breakfast, but I manage to hold it together.

We eagerly plant our boots on the ground at Al-Taqaddum Airbase at 1000 hours. They put us up in temporary housing (crappy cloth tents), but at least there is electricity and nice shower trailers nearby. This is home for a few days until we board a CH-46 Sea Knight chopper for a fifteen-minute flight east to Camp Fallujah.

The 2–136th Infantry Battalion is spread across Iraq. Bravo Company is assigned to Camp Fallujah, a Marine base in the very heart of insurgent territory west of Baghdad with CPT Daniel Murphy and 1st SGT Richard Eggert, and most of the rest are left at Al Taqaddum Air Base. Montero and Steinbach are part of a group that heads off to Balad Air Base forty miles north of Baghdad on the Tigris River. Will Bernhjelm, Scott Sherwood, Matt Larson, and a bunch of my other friends from Alpha Company get attached to a unit from the active Army's 4th Infantry Division at Camp Liberty. They patrol the streets near the city of Abu Ghraib.

The Marines tell us Camp Fallujah is quite a bit better than TQ. I certainly hope so because this place is a barren slab of shit, dried powder shit. The only bright spot is the chow hall, which is nothing short of spectacular, even better than back at Buehring. A few of us jump on a shuttle to the "big" PX on the other side of camp, roughly twelve miles from one end to the other with nothing in between except wreckage from the war—bombed out buildings, destroyed MIGs (Soviet fighter jets), and open desert. Their so-called PX is not much. They are out of Q-tips, an essential tool to keep the brown desert dust out of your ears, so the trip is pretty much a waste of my time. The wind is non-stop forty-plus mph kicking up the worst sandstorm that you could imagine; of course, I left my Oakley sunglasses in my computer bag so my eyes are killing me in seconds.

We're told that Camp TQ is shelled by mortars every week; that certainly adds to the adventure. The area from Baghdad west through Fallujah and TQ to Ramadi, then northeast to Tikrit forms what is called the Sunni Triangle, our home for the next year. The Sunni Triangle extends roughly 125 miles along each leg and encompasses several major population centers including Fallujah, Baqubah, Baghdad, Ramadi, Tikrit, and Samarra. The area is home to many of Saddam Hussein's Sunni supporters and is where he was captured on December 13, 2003, in the village of ad-Dawr, fifteen miles south of Tikrit. We learn that Camp Fallujah's front gate was hit by RPGs (rocket propelled grenades) earlier this week. *Very inviting.*

The chow hall is a sanctuary from the harsh reality of what goes on here. There are plenty of television sets with sports games from the night before (we are eight hours ahead of U.S. Central time), and all the food you want, even an ice cream stand. In the chow hall you rarely hear conversation about missions, the danger of being over here, or anything of that nature. Best of all you don't hear the constant, rhythmic rapping of attack helicopters flying overhead searching for insurgents, nonstop airplane traffic, or sporadic gunfire and mortar rounds exploding.

People are laughing, joking around, and telling stories about home. It's not until we walk outside that reality punches us in the face. The first things we see are bombed out former Iraqi Army Barracks and pock-marked concrete walls surrounding the chow hall. Then I feel the pulsating rotors almost before I hear the roar of the big choppers, punctuated sporadically by gunfire from patrols test-firing their weapons before they leave the gate or, as we say, go outside the wire (the camp is completely surrounded by razor wire much like a prison).

Back at the tent, it's time to relax with a quick game of MLB 06 on my Sony PlayStation portable when I hear a series of explosions. Even with my headphones playing, I hear and feel two sharp blasts. I rip off the headphones just in time to hear three more that sound farther away. SGT Marshall Tanner is watching a movie on his laptop, also with his headphones. "Did you hear that bang?" he asks. "What the fuck was that?"

I am pretty sure that those were incoming mortar rounds, and the piercing tone bellowing out of the base loud speakers followed quickly by a chilling voice announcing, "INCOMING ... INCOMING ... INCOMING" erases all doubt. We all just stay in the tent, make a few sick jokes, and try to act like it is nothing unusual. Unfortunately, we discover soon enough just how true that is; mortar attacks are daily events, not at all unusual. We're told if we can't get into a shelter quickly that the chances of being hit by mortar increase when you go running around; so, we stay put. I'm not sure I understand the logic, but hopefully they're right. We're done training; it's the real deal, now.

Chapter 10

WELCOME TO CAMP FALLUJAH

Saturday, April 8, 2006

Seven years of training, a painful week of good-byes, fifteen hours in the air from Camp Shelby, nine days in Kuwait, and here we are, boots on the ground, at Camp Fallujah, Iraq, ready for war, ready to kick some insurgent ass.

Okay, the ground is more like brown baby powder and it's almost impossible to tell friend from foe among the Iraqis. The bad guys don't wear uniforms like real soldiers; they hide in plain sight among the locals who are too terrified to point them out. They pop out and blow you away with their stupid car bombs or buried improvised explosive devices (IEDs), and they couldn't care less if they kill Iraqi kids, elders, or mothers as long as they maintain control through terror. They think they can intimidate us into leaving or just wait until we lose interest in saving people from being sucked back into the Middle Ages.

We're not in Camp Shelby, Kosovo, or Kuwait. Those places were vacations; this is hell. Just walking into our temporary housing tent is a slap of reality as a shredded canvas wall flaps in our faces.

Outside is wreckage of the next tent, it was annihilated by a mortar shell a couple days ago. God, if they can hit that one, they can hit us. Hopefully, we will move into our permanent, concrete building soon.

This is Mesopotamia, where the three wise men began their walk across this same brown talcum powder two thousand years ago to see Baby Jesus, and it is where Adam and Eve began our civilization long before Christ, Mohammad, or any of us, existed. One can only wonder whatever happened to civilization, and where are the wise men?

Mixed into our training on desert survival, bomb and combatant identification, Rules of Engagement, and cultural awareness, we get a briefing on local history. "Mesopotamia" is a Greek word for "the land between the rivers"; in this case the Tigris and Euphrates rivers, no match for the lush green forests separating the Mississippi and St. Croix rivers back home, but these rivers certainly have an impressive history.

It is said that civilization found its genesis in Iraq five thousand years before Christ and was home to the first written words; actually, that early writing was primarily a system of drawings. In addition to being the first to write, ancient Mesopotamians were among the first to build libraries, study astronomy (before the Greeks), and explore mathematical context. They created a numeral system that is said to be the source of the sixty-minute hour, twenty-four-hour day, and the 360-degree circle, as well as creating remarkably accurate mathematical formulas. And, three prominent religions trace their history to this region—Christianity, Islam, and Judaism. Perhaps that strength also is the region's greatest obstacle to peace, learning to live in harmony even with seven thousand years of experience.

It may be the cradle of civilization and home to major religions, but you have to ask yourself *what is God's plan?* This place has been ravaged by war for centuries, and there is no end in sight. People who have difficulty even telling their own friends and enemies apart are filled with hatred for one another. Soldiers undoubtedly have pondered that strange dilemma since before Christ or Mohammed appeared.

The Tigris and Euphrates rivers tumble from the rugged Zagros and Taurus mountains that stretch from Iraq's northern border with Iran along the Turkish border to Syria and the vast Arabian Desert. At the base of the mountains, the rivers provide a brief oasis that quickly evaporates into the baked, arid dust of the parched desert expanse. For centuries nomadic tribes have chased the elusive greener pastures that move across the region with the seasons. They tend sheep, goats, and camels, while traveling on foot, as their ancestors have for centuries, from the lush northern mountain fields south to the lowland river pastures during the winter wet season and retreating to the mountains again when summer heat steals the moisture. Massive winter snows in the mountains have stymied armies for all of history and poured life into the rivers each spring. With such dramatic seasonal shifts, nomadic farmers long ago devised an extraordinary system of canals and storage ponds to divert and retain much of the life-sustaining liquid throughout the farmland, creating the world's first irrigation system.

Giant pumping stations pull water from the canals to quench the thirst of Iraq's cities even today. The pumping stations are not merely big wells, but are major military outposts complete with living quarters and observation towers designed as defensive fortresses. One of our tasks is to defend two such pumping stations, Pump House Barney and Pump House Flanders, which provide water to Fallujah, a city of three hundred thousand people, and Camp Fallujah where we live with fifteen thousand Marines and a few soldiers. Western Iraq is nearly void of stone or wood for building; thus, construction is virtually all concrete or mud huts with a sprinkling of imported materials.

Fallujah, a stronghold for supporters of Saddam Hussein's Bathist regime, had largely avoided major conflict in the war until March 31, 2004, when four U.S. contractors were murdered and their bodies were hung on a bridge over the Euphrates River in an act of public defiance that was televised worldwide. U.S. forces pounded suspected insurgent strongholds with airstrikes throughout the summer and early fall. On November 8, a massive force of more than ten thousand American troops aided by two thousand Iraqi Army members launched Operation Phantom Fury directly into the city, searching house by house for the enemy. It was estimated that seventy to ninety percent of the city's three hundred thousand residents had fled.

Primary objectives for Operation Phantom Fury were to flush out the estimated three thousand hardcore insurgents entrenched in the city and to encourage residents to return to participate in the country's elections scheduled for January 2005. The overwhelming American force cleared the city, and people poured back amid the staggering task of repairing and rebuilding half of the city's 39,000 houses.

Back at camp we were briefed on the success of the operation, but all I want to do is call Katie to wish her Happy Birthday. Just my luck, all the phones are shut off for the day. Nobody tells us why, but that usually means somebody was killed and they don't want us calling out until the family is notified.

The only thing keeping me sane today is a computer program loaded with old Nintendo games. I've played Zelda trying to keep my mind off home, but I miss Katie, my boys, EVERYBODY, and EVERYTHING, so much. I turn on my computer and listen to a song, and it reminds me of something I was doing back home. I watch a movie and laugh, but Katie's not here to laugh with me. In this room full of some of the closest friends I'll ever have, I feel alone. The toughest part of this job isn't leaving the wire and heading into danger, it is realizing what you left at home.

Everything will be much better when we move into our real barracks. We don't even have our rucks and duffel bags. All I have is a carry-on bag, and it contains nothing but electronics. Not good planning, but at least we have a place to sleep.

I slept like shit last night, but tonight should be better if only because I am dead tired. I am used to having a pillow but mine is packed away in my ruck somewhere in storage. The only thing that

I have to use is my body armor, which is one degree short of being a rock even after I pull out the SAPI plates. It's actually a cool night in the desert so we flip the heat on because nobody has blankets or sleeping bags, but during the night some dumbass under the heater turns on the air conditioner. I wake up freezing, flip the heat back on, and warn him if he touches that dial again, the enemy will be the least of his problems. He doesn't touch it.

I'm sound asleep at two a.m. when a tremendously loud series of paralyzing cracks pierce the silence of the night, followed by "whooshing" sounds sucking the air from camp, jerking us all to full alert.

We knew the dangers coming here, but suddenly talking about war at Camp Shelby strikes me as something totally different than actually feeling, hearing, and smelling real bombs that are searching for my bed. Holy shit! It's weird to suddenly feel that people I don't even know are lurking just outside the wire trying to kill me. No amount of training prepares you for this moment of realization punctuated by incoming mortar shells and the sound, fury, and feel of real artillery shells being launched. Being new to the war zone, we are uncertain for just a moment whether it is incoming or outgoing bombs. Quickly we learn it's our guys blasting away in retaliation for an insurgent mortar attack. My introduction to Shock and Awe.

Incoming bombs activate instant response from our highly sophisticated radar tracking system that seeks out the bomb's heat signature, tracing back to the launch point and hurling huge-ass artillery shells down on the mortar tube location. The cacophony of battle registers about 5.5 on the Richter scale, jolting everyone awake; and then as quickly as it started the all-clear sounds followed by silence almost as loud as the explosions. Eventually, I drift off to sleep, but it's not sound sleep. Sleeping has never been a problem for me, but suddenly the slightest movement or whisper or noise and I bolt to full alert. Welcome to the war zone.

After my shortened night, a little free time gives me an opportunity to explore the post, and I quickly discover that it's not too bad. The main area, where we will be living, has a decent PX, chow hall, and some real trees, a great luxury in Iraq. It's amazing what a difference a little vegetation makes. TQ has no trees as far as the eye can see, assuming the air is calm enough to see. There is nothing but flat, baked dust, but at Camp Fallujah we have palm trees. It's not quite as depressing when you have something to look at other than sand and dung beetles. The camp is enormous with living and work quarters clustered on interior sites surrounded by vast areas of open desert inside solid walls that reach high into the sky, making attacks virtually impossible and creating extreme difficulty for anyone attempting to drop a mortar shell on target—any hits are pure luck.

Our rooms are small, but at least we finally have indoor plumbing and air conditioning, pretty essential when air temperature often touches 130 degrees.

We zero in our weapons at Camp Fallujah at least once a month. The last thing you want in a firefight is to discover that your weapons are not sighted in.

WELCOME TO CAMP FALLUJAH

We get our mission—Camp Force Protection. Sounds boring, a waste of time, but we all realize that camp security is essential. We spend the first month providing security inside camp at the seventeen observation towers (boring) then rotate to cover the three entry control points (also boring). Finally, we go outside the wire, but barely, as we drive through nearby villages performing perimeter security. The closest we come to action is a brief foray out the South Gate into the nearby village of Al Mehr. These folks are literally a stone's throw from camp and know if anyone attacks us, they live in the first place we will look. They're not particularly friendly, just cooperative as anyone caught helpless in the teeth of war would be.

On a good note, I finally talk to Katie and the boys. I wish her a belated Happy Birthday, and immediately remember what I left behind. God help anyone who tries to get in the way of me making it back to my family in one piece.

Our platoon is summoned to the main point to get new improved SAPI plates and side SAPI plates for our body armor. Where there used to be an unprotected area under our arms, there is a full plate of armor that greatly improves the chance of surviving an IED attack. Some idiots are whining about how heavy it is, but for me anything that keeps us safer is worth it. There are plenty of other armies that only wish they had half of the armor U.S. soldiers wear, and we have idiots whining that we have too much.

Tomorrow, Horn, Nelson, and I will be going on patrol with the guys we are scheduled to replace. The plan is for us to shadow them for the next few days, take a day off, and head out for ten days, protecting Pump House Barney, a water treatment facility that has been attacked at least once a week for the past month. As the source of all of the water for Camp Fallujah, protecting Barney is crucial.

Excitement at our first real mission outside the wire evaporates when we arrive at the compound all geared up and ready to go only to be greeted with news that our mission has been scrubbed. An IED was spotted on the only road to the pump house and a nasty firefight erupted just outside the South Gate within the past hour, which I heard before we left our tent. No way is the commander about to throw a bunch of rookies into this situation.

Disappointed, Marshall Tanner, Randy Fish, Jimmy Wosika, and I head off to learn how to operate the Backscatter vehicle scanning system, a relatively simple concept that employs high-tech equipment stuffed into a very nondescript truck similar to a standard vanilla U-haul. It conceals a high-powered x-ray system that scans vehicles and pedestrians entering Camp for weapons, bombs, or any kind of nuclear radiation.

Chapter 11

OUTSIDE 'THE WIRE' AT LAST

Horn, Nelly, and I escape the wire on our first patrol; although it's relatively uneventful, we do find a moment of excitement. As our convoy of three up armored Humvees and a seven-ton troop carrier departs the gate, a Marine sergeant tells us some kids are stopping traffic on our route and he warns that, the last time this happened, an IED was spotted there.

Turning onto the road, we spot a dilapidated, white pickup truck, vehicle of choice for insurgents, on the left side of the road and two men standing on a berm two hundred meters to the right. To limit exposure, only one troop dismounts from each vehicle for a twenty-five meter initial IED sweep. Finding nothing, they signal for the rest of us to dismount and walk along the road, searching for anything out of the ordinary. I move to the right, focusing on the two suspicious men. One appears to be talking on a cell phone; the other is motioning toward us, setting off a giant red flag waving inside my head. With every gun trained on the Iraqis, two of our guys cautiously move up the berm and search the civilians. There is no cell phone, and they have nothing illegal on them, but they definitely appear jumpy.

The area is known to be littered with IEDs; obviously, even if these guys had nothing to do with planting the bombs, at the very least, they probably know who did, but they won't talk. Holding a steady bead on them with my M4 carbine as we move away, I realize they resemble the pop-up targets at the firing range; it would be an easy shot. In the end we discover this was not such a dangerous situation; in fact, it's rather routine, but it definitely provides an introduction to live combat where lives are on the line, demanding split-second decisions. Your senses intensify, and you become alert to every little sight, sound, and movement realizing that even the most subtle, innocuous change could be a lurking serpent ready to strike any unsuspecting soldier or helpless farmer caught in conflict.

Returning to Camp Fallujah I want to call home, but another attack on one of our patrols has injured thirteen Marines and killed one, shutting down the phones and computers. After dinner artillery fire streaks out from camp in retaliation for another mortar attack, and the roar of outgoing bombs is relentless. Everybody in Camp wants to go kill the scum that attacked our guys, but we settle for the deafening roar of our artillery blasting away, raining monstrous bombs on them. The sweet sound of justice.

Seven loud explosions shake the ground, stopping me in my tracks; apparently the insurgents aren't intimidated and don't plan to celebrate Good Friday. The piercing scream of the incoming alarm confirms that it is indeed incoming bombs. Again, we don't bother going to the bunkers. It's too late, not a particularly comforting thought when we look at the pile of rubble that used to be the next tent.

Once the mayhem ceases, McDonough and I head out to eat and come upon a giant swarm of killer bees hanging on the side of one of the cement buildings where we are scheduled to live. The swarm is the size of a basketball and they are all pissed off, apparently they don't care for mortar attacks, either. We give them wide berth.

Rystad comes up and warns us not to go back to the tents. Intelligence reports and the recent pattern of mortar attacks indicate a high probability of more attacks on the south portion of camp where we live. He adds that body armor must be worn at all times until at least 1900 hours tonight. We grab some chow and head back to the Morale, Welfare, and Recreation Center to enjoy a game of college football on PlayStation. We don't get back to the tent until almost 2200.

Bradley Fighting Vehicle on security near Pump House Barney

Our Humvee parked at a sheik's house

Here's my buddy Cringer, named for the cowardly green tiger in
the "He-Man" cartoons that becomes the powerful, courageous
Battle Cat with a touch from the Grayskull sword.

On patrol in the tall grass along River Road by the
Euphrates River near the sheik's house

Chapter 12

DEFENDING
PUMP HOUSE BARNEY

Another week guarding camp passes quietly before we roll outside the wire once more. No more Rules of Engagement classes, no more briefings. SSG David Hammac's squad escorts us to Pump House Barney where Nelson, Horn, and McDonough fill me in on all the shenanigans I've missed. No serious action other than celebrating Easter with the Iraqi Army guys who are up for a party any time, even if it's a Christian holiday. For Easter dinner, Nelson sent the Iraqi Security Force guys to the market across the canal for a live chicken that they killed, defeathered, and cooked.

We're barely settled in when a mortar round explodes fifty yards outside the wall. Glancing down the road, we spot the suspect launch vehicle stopped in traffic, but we don't have a clear shot without risk of injuring innocent people. A quick call to Marine Headquarters Group (MHG) requesting a Quick Reactionary Force team is denied, which makes no sense. Now we're having second thoughts about holding fire. The Rules of Engagement state that if there is "reasonable certainty" that the target was involved in the attack, deadly force is authorized. We have no doubt that this truck launched the mortars or, at the very least, participated in the deed.

Vehicle of choice for hit-and-run mortar attacks is the Bongo, a flatbed truck with a bed that can be raised like the box on a dump truck enabling insurgents to adjust the angle of their mortar tube, the poor man's artillery gun. Fortunately, their need for speed to escape retaliation by our artillery generally results in lousy accuracy; the flatbed trucks are easy bombing targets for our attack helicopters and counter-battery artillery guns.

The three soldiers/marines who man the Pump House towers are on four-hour shifts along with a sergeant of the guard (SOG). At the moment Nelson, Horn, and I are the only ones available for SOG; so, we are on eight-hour shifts to ensure that a SOG is always on duty, keeping the guys vigilant and making the final decision to fire or not when a threat arises. I draw the crappy night shift, 2200–0600 hours. The enemy rarely, if ever, attacks at night since they have no night vision capabilities. They know we own the night.

**Showing off my guns and tattoos on guard in the main tower
of Pump House Flanders**

DEFENDING PUMP HOUSE BARNEY

Night shift introduces me to working directly with the Iraqi Security Force (ISF), and it comes with a heavy dose of apprehension. I decide to maintain a mental wall between us. For all I know, they are gathering intelligence for a future attack—a heightened concern when I discover two of them were in the Iraqi Army under Saddam Hussein, although they claim their lives are much better now. Iraqi soldiers don't live at Camp Fallujah; they just appear for duty at the Pump House, stay for a week, and then melt back into the desert. That makes us even more uncertain about them.

Hassan, the ISF leader, is the equivalent of an American platoon sergeant, although he has been told to take all his orders from the three NCOs in my squad. He is a skinny, little guy only about five-feet-five and as goofy as you could make someone, but if one of his guys is doing anything wrong, he fixes the problem in a second. Hassan harbors deep hatred for Saddam Hussein, claiming the Iraqi Army castrated him. He is the only one I come close to trusting. I say come close because I will not allow myself to actually trust any of them. The rest of them are pretty much a ragtag bunch of clowns with little or no training. Putting guns in their hands is very unnerving; I never turn my back on them.

Jahmeed is my least favorite of the ISF guys; so, my first night working as SOG on the late shift, I head up to Tower Two to check on him and Cpl. Daniel Logan (the Marine attached to my team). Logan and I are talking when Jahmeed tries to show us bestiality porn videos on his cell phone. We were both like "What is wrong with this guy?"

A few nights later, I'm SOG on perimeter patrol when SPC Nick Maurstad radios to me from Tower Two. "Kries, Jahmeed is freaking out. He's screaming that he sees Ali Baba (their word for bad guy), and he's getting ready to start shooting into the darkness."

As I arrive Maurstad is forcing Jahmeed to look into the darkness through his night vision goggles. I check out the area with my thermal scope, which senses even the slightest body heat from a person or animal. Nothing, no movement, or warm bodies of any sort.

To eliminate any doubt I call Bravo X-ray and request that they fire illumination rounds over the fields south of the pump house. Illumination rounds explode in the air, unleashing brilliant, white, glowing fireballs similar to gigantic welding torches floating slowly to the earth on parachutes, turning the landscape to high noon. That convinces Jahmeed that there are no "Ali Baba" in the area, and reassures anyone who might be worried.

Uneasy with this wired whacko, I grab Jahmeed's AK-47, just to make sure he doesn't freak out and kill someone, and order him out of the tower because he is worthless to us. He refuses to leave, warning me that he needs to keep watch because Ali Baba is coming. Fine, at least he appears relatively calm now and I have his weapon. I slip out and no more than enter the SOG shack when Maurstad calls in panic, "Sergeant Kriesel, he's freaking out again."

I've had enough of Jahmeed's shit so I grab some string and a couple of chemlights (military version of snap lights, similar to what kids hang on their necks for Halloween). I attach the chemlights to the string, creating a necklace that can be seen for miles in the absolute darkness of the desert. Back in the tower, I hand the necklace to Jahmeed and order him to put it on. He slides it over his head and his eyes flash with fear as he realizes he has just become a lighthouse beacon flashing across the landscape from the rooftop of the pump house in the heart of the treacherous Anbar Province. He freaks out, screaming that he can be seen by snipers far away and could get shot. He's terrified and wants to get out of the tower—exactly what I intended. As Jahmeed slithers away to his room, I tell Hassan that I won't allow any crazed, undisciplined Iraqis in my watchtowers freaking out and distracting my men.

The other ISF guys seem all right, and they work hard to get us to like them, but Jahmeed definitely has tarnished Iraqi–American relations at Pump House Barney and they know it. The rest of the day, two ISF guys are always with Jahmeed when he is in the tower, they don't trust him, either. They are constantly watching the area outside the tower so closely that they notice even the slightest movement. The only advantage they bring is that they know who belongs in the area and who does not, and they are quick to spot anything that is out of the ordinary.

Initially, the Iraqi Security Force guys stay overnight at Barney, but as time passes and relations are strained, they become infrequent visitors. After a few weeks they disappear altogether; apparently somebody at headquarters realized it was a bad idea putting them in our quarters in the first place. Once they depart we rip out their disgusting bunks, disinfect the room, and build new bunks for our guys and a storage area for chow.

Returning to Camp after a week at Pump House Barney, we are back guarding the towers on the camp perimeter. This is by far the most boring duty I have had in more than seven years in the Army; okay, guarding the power plant in Minnesota was pretty close.

After our mind-numbing shift, McDonough and I grab something to eat and are heading back to our quarters when we encounter the first sergeant. "Show me your tourniquet, soldier," he spits at McDonough. We had just been given orders that everyone must carry a tourniquet in his right pocket at all times, but McDonough didn't have one because he was at Pump House Barney when that information came out.

"Who is your Sergeant?" he bellows. I step forward with no problem, taking responsibility, as I bite my tongue and accept his reprimand. In my mind he is a poor excuse for a leader and that thought is only reinforced when it is reported that he once said, "I love to bust soldiers." So, there are no tears or farewell festivities when he is fired and reassigned.

Right now I am totally frustrated, not sure why I re-enlisted. I volunteered for Iraq so I could do my part, but all we are doing here is sitting in the Camp towers and guarding entry control points (ECP) while the Marines do all the real work. The Marines don't want this job so they conned the Army into giving us up and sticking us with it. I came here to fight terrorists, but I'm nothing but a glorified security guard. Bravo Company is a band of highly trained fighters with all the best equipment, and we are sitting in reserve. It makes about as much sense as keeping Brett Favre or Peyton Manning on the bench in a Super Bowl.

Chapter 13

TAKING THE BATTLE TO THE INSURGENTS

Our Army and Air Force guys are pounding the hell out of the insurgents in Fallujah day and night; but as vermin will do, the rats start leaking out of the city into our neighborhood, planting more and more, bigger and bigger IEDs and launching maniacal suicide attacks on our patrols at the pump houses. Injuries are rapidly depleting the number of Marines available for patrol.

In response to the growing threat, Camp Fallujah's new Marine Headquarters Group Commander, COL George Bristol, is looking to increase patrols. That's when he discovers a highly trained, fully mechanized infantry company right before his eyes, guarding towers while our heavily armored fighting vehicles sit in storage collecting dust, the Minnesota National Guard's Bravo Company, 2–136th Infantry.

The insurgent rats keep getting bolder and bolder, attacking patrols and tossing mortars into Camp every day now. Colonel Bristol has had enough. When CPT Chip Rankin, a high school teacher and wrestling coach from Litchfield, Minnesota, arrives to take command of Bravo Company, he and Colonel Bristol devise a plan to cut down attacks on the Camp—hell, we should at least be able to eat, sleep, and relax in relative safety.

"So, how do we keep them from attacking Camp Fallujah?" Colonel Bristol asks at a senior staff meeting. Simple, don't let them get close to Camp. Well, maybe not so simple, but a worthy objective. Enemy mortars have a range of roughly seven thousand meters (four to five miles). So, the primary task is to clear a seven-mile buffer zone around Camp Fallujah. The only way to accomplish that task is to implement aggressive patrols, check vehicles, stop suspicious citizens, collect better intelligence, and bust down doors.

Camp Fallujah is a Marine base, and we aren't even active army; so, some of the macho Marines have serious problems with "citizen soldiers" in combat; although interestingly, it is only those who have never left the wire who hassle us, the ones who go outside the wire give us plenty of respect because they know what it's like out there; especially Colonel Bristol. Bristol is the epitome of what a leader should be, with thirty years experience and on his third tour in Iraq.

It doesn't take Bristol long to put his Army National Guard company to work. Slowly at first, we go out on patrol, real missions checking the roads, visiting villages, and busting down doors where there are reports of suspected insurgent activity. Danger spikes enormously the second you venture outside the wire, but we came to Iraq to change that, to make a difference.

Some days we can be doing town searches in the scorching desert with everybody, including the Marines, whining and bitching about the heat, the incessant brown powder filling our lungs, and the need to keep marching hour after hour. It sucks. *Why are we doing this?* Suddenly there's Colonel Bristol, a six-foot-eight mechanized mountain, and SGT Maj. Walter O'Connell, carrying bigger assault packs than anyone else, running past us to the front of the line. Everybody shuts their mouth and marches on with pride just to be one of Bristol's guys.

Okay, as much as I want to get into the action and make a difference, I quickly realize action comes with risk, risk that is about to hit high gear. My squad and two squads from 3rd Platoon are assigned to a quick reactionary force team. We are the military equivalent of the fire department sent in to backup, rescue, or reinforce units that get into any sort of predicament outside the wire. The unit we are replacing suffered five casualties yesterday in a sustained firefight, something of a rarity for the insurgent cowards who prefer to plant IEDs or take an occasional sniper shot; but they rarely engage in actual sustained battle. Working as on-base security guards seemed to be a joke at first, but we soon discover it's merely the Marines way of having us take baby steps before launching into real war, and giving them a chance to check us out.

There are three levels, ingeniously dubbed QRF 1, QRF 2, and QRF 3, with QRF 1, staging at the QRF building, always ready to deploy within five minutes. Each shift is twelve hours. We're on QRF 2, when QRF 1 is called to escort an Iraqi Army soldier back to Pump House Barney, requiring us to report to the QRF building, or, as we call it, "the firehouse." At 2000 hours they roll out as we move to the firehouse.

Within minutes we learn that QRF 1 hit an IED, suffering two wounded. Our job—get there ASAP. This is our first serious action, and I am commanding the lead vehicle with Nelson and Horn in charge of the second and third vehicles, and I definitely don't want to screw this up.

Being unfamiliar with the roads and navigating to the blast site only heightens the anxiety. My heart pounds and nerves chatter, but it's a good nervous condition that forces me to focus intensely because we're working against the clock with guys depending on us. As we approach the IED blast site, we are ordered to return to the South Gate to escort an ambulance. Why didn't they tell us about the ambulance before valuable time was wasted? Annoyed, we race back to the gate for the medics, but they just sit there.

"Aren't you transporting them?" one of the nervous medics asks.

"Hell, no, you are. Follow us. We're no taxi service; we're your security."

Five minutes later we are on scene, expecting the worst; you always expect the worst, especially when you hear that two are wounded. It's dark and the first person I spot is SGT Matthew Johnson, Bravo Team leader from SSG Kerry Mandt's squad. Johnson is sweating and visibly shaking.

"That was fucking loud!" Johnson blurts and then calms down enough to fill me in. Their three-vehicle convoy was traveling along Route California when guys in the first vehicle spotted a black strip across the road, but it was too late. They swerved but hit the strip, detonating four 120mm mortar rounds buried under the road.

SGT Matthew Bye, Alpha Team leader, was sitting "shotgun" in the lead vehicle. He suffered what turns out to be a broken right femur and has a chunk of shrapnel imbedded in his left femur, with open fractures on his right hand. He is medivaced out of Iraq.

The driver, SPC Scott Stroud, appears to have a broken right foot, but it turns out to be less serious. After the blast, Stroud climbed up on the vehicle and removed the fifty-caliber machine gun to avoid any risk of it falling into enemy hands. He then tried to load Bye into the ambulance before the medics saw Stroud's injuries and told him to sit down and relax.

On arrival I ground guide my vehicle between the ambulance on the right side of the road and the destroyed Hummer on the left; that's a maneuver in a tight area where you put a soldier outside your vehicle to guide you so that you don't run over anybody or anything (like an IED). We do this because sight lines, or the lack thereof, and mirrors don't provide adequate close-up view. I push aside the gunner's shield that was blown off their vehicle and realize that it most likely saved Stroud's life.

Medics are loading the wounded as we pass, but I am determined not to be distracted for even a quick look. My responsibility is to remain constantly vigilant to spot and shoot insurgent snipers. We pass the carnage, assume far side security, and keep scanning the area for movement. We don't see anyone, but I'm ninety-nine percent certain that they are out there watching, taking pride in their dirty deed, and studying how we react.

It doesn't fully hit me until we are pulling security later that one of our guys is going home, and if we had been QRF 1, it would have been me in the right front seat instead of Bye and that would be me in the ambulance. If there had been one more stupid call before 2000 hours, it would have been my vehicle that was blown up. I'm not worried so much about what would have happened to me, as I am terrified by what would have happened to Katie if she had gotten that call.

McDonough checks out a gun seized in a village search

Some of the insurgent weapons Bravo Company captured in October

Sharing a few minutes with boys while taking census in nearby villages—apparently not everyone sends in their census forms there either

Cute Iraqi boy pops a salute

Getting ready for another mission, we all paint on eye black,
just to look a tad more intimidating

Tell the folks back home we touched the Euphrates—
SPC John Albert, SPC Matt Pietzak, and SPC Stephen Perry

Chapter 14

BACK TO PUMP HOUSE BARNEY

In July, Bravo Company happily relinquishes tower watch duty to the Marines. Our company is stretched thin right now with a quarter of us rotating through a place called Habbniyah, 15 km west, near Ramadi; mostly our Bradley tank crews try to keep the route to Ramadi clear.

While on patrol in Habbaniya, SGT Bryan Kutter, a Bradley gunner, was shot through the arm with the bullet striking the armor on his neck, preventing more serious injury. The Bradleys are taking small arms fire and RPG (rocket propelled grenade) blasts almost nonstop, and although reactive armor thwarts most attacks, one Bradley was completely destroyed. Luckily the crew was able to abandon ship before suffering serious injuries.

The Bradleys are constantly on patrol throughout the summer of 2006, keeping supply routes clear of IEDs in the Ramadi area where Al Qaeda has established headquarters in a futile attempt to cut off supplies to the U.S. troops and to avoid losing Ramadi to the Americans; it doesn't work.

Two days ago our company hit three IEDs and found a vehicle borne IED (VBIED) before it detonated. Again, no serious injuries.

This company is the luckiest bunch of bastards I've ever seen. We've had more action than the rest of the brigade combined but only two people have gone to Germany for medical treatment. Nobody has been killed.

We're finishing up another week at Pump House Barney at 1400 hours when two mortar rounds explode five hundred meters from our position. SPC Michael Neumiller is freaking out because he can't spot the insurgents—not surprising when you realize their mortars have a range of up to seven thousand meters. The bombs land far enough away from us that it's no big deal, except to Neumiller. We go about our business as normal, and I take over the shift at 1930 hours. God, I hope we're not getting so accustomed to attack that we lose our edge. A little bit of fear is good to keep you alert.

I'm in the tower, scanning the area when Bravo X-ray calls and calmly advises me to stand alert for an incoming round; then he casually counts down from eight. The way he talks leads me to believe that it is our artillery from Camp Fallujah firing on the village across the canal, and they want us to serve as forward observers relaying impact effectiveness and accuracy details.

I grab my binoculars and assume a position in the doorway of the tower where I have maximum view of the surrounding area when, suddenly, a terrifying "zing" rips past, followed instantly by a deafening explosion not more than 40 meters away. The concussion vibrates the tower violently; instinctively I dive to the deck.

Confused and dazed I pick myself up from the floor just as Nelson comes racing up from the SOG room and I tell him Bravo X-ray had given me a ten-second warning about artillery rounds they were firing. Nelly grabs the radio and shouts so loud they may have heard him back at Fallujah without it: "BRAVO X-RAY, THIS IS PUMP HOUSE BARNEY, THAT ROUND JUST HIT OUR OUTER WALL, END MISSION. END FIRE MISSION. YOU'RE PUTTING IT RIGHT ON US!"

No response.

In the distance six blasts launch the big bombs, definitely 155mm artillery rising up from Camp Fallujah, followed closely by six more, and we're paralyzed by the thought that we are about to be vaporized in a storm of "friendly fire." Seconds later a series of colossal clouds erupts from the village across the canal to our southwest and we exhale.

The radio is messed up so Bravo X-ray calls us on the satellite phone, continuing his calm demeanor as he casually explains that the first two blasts were not "friendly" fire. He was just warning us of incoming hostile rounds. Nelly, in not such a calm manner, suggests that future communications should be much more specific before he gets us killed.

The round that hit our position was enemy; our GOC (ground operations center) recently installed upgraded radar to track incoming mortars targeting the pump houses and had called to warn us without taking time to explain who fired the incoming round. The instant the enemy launches a mortar round, our radar system captures grid coordinates of the launch site, feeds them to the computer, and within thirty seconds the 155mm cannons unleash a crippling counterattack. The artillery fire we heard was twelve rounds of 155mm punishing the spot where somebody fired at us. Hopefully they annihilated the bastards, but usually those sneaky little snakes fire from a dusty, white pickup truck, and then they are gone almost before their bombs make impact. We talk to the GOC and get the confusion ironed out. For future reference it is agreed that Bravo X-ray will clearly tell us when there is incoming enemy fire.

Nelly spends the next month giving me shit about standing in the tower with my binoculars watching the enemy mortar rounds come at us; it was all pretty funny after the fact.

I'm trying to relax between shifts at Barney when Nelson bolts into the SOG quarters announcing that Pump House Flanders just took a direct hit from an RPG, injuring Sergeants Chad Hassel and Randy Fish. Hassel suffered only a mild headache, but Fish, one of my roommates, took shrapnel to the arm.

All hell breaks loose a few days later at Pump House Flanders when two dump trucks reinforced with sandbags and steel plates roll up along the canal, carrying forty crazy insurgents who are smiling and waving until they pull parallel to the towers. They unleash an onslaught of machine gun and small arms fire, AK47s and grenades. Normally staffed by a squad of twelve to fifteen soldiers and marines, Flanders has only ten defenders who are suddenly under attack from three directions.

Pinned down by sustained, massive firepower from the insurgents, SSG David Hammac slips outside the Pump House to engage the enemy and check on his men in the towers. Early in the battle, SPC Jared Moe suffers shrapnel wounds and is given first aid by Spcs. John Olson, Matthew Generux, and Charles Knetter, while bullets slam into the walls beside them. They barely finish treating Moe's wounds when an injured Marine literally tumbles into their room. After treating his wounds, they grab their rifles and join the fight.

SPC Jasen Klimek races to Tower One where he and SPC Domingo Augilar fire their M16 rifles and 50-caliber machine guns and toss grenades at the insurgents with little more than a pile of sandbags and a sheet of bulletproof glass the size of a windshield for protection.

SPC Billy Feragen turns his 50-caliber machine gun on the enemy and lays down a barrage of fire while SGT Joe Mehlhorn grabs the tower radio, summoning help from Camp Fallujah. Insurgents are so close to the pump house that calling in the heavy guns from Fallujah brings a high risk for friendly fire casualties, but a risk that needs to be taken in the face of an advancing, overwhelming enemy force. Bravo Company soldiers continue firing and launching grenades, hoping to hold off the advancing enemy soldiers and to disable the dump trucks before the insurgents escape from Fallujah's big guns.

SGT David Olson grabs all the ammunition he can carry from the ammunition storage room and darts across the open court area to Tower One, returns, and carries more ammo to Tower Three all the while dodging a firestorm of bullets. Once the towers are resupplied, he mans a 50-caliber machine gun until learning the soldiers in Tower Two are running low on ammunition. Olson races to the storage area for more ammo where he discovers that Camp Fallujah is about to launch mortar shells at the insurgents less than fifty meters outside the pump house walls. He's told to take cover but runs to Tower Two with the ammo and warns his buddies, "Incoming artillery!"

Tension escalates another notch when Mehlhorn is told that forward observers are concerned that they may not have the targets zeroed in very well.

"Here they come, everybody!" Mehlhorn shouts the instant Fallujah fires the big guns, "Get down. Get down. Get down!"

The blasts are precise, destroying the trucks and turning the tide of the 38-minute battle. The warriors of Pump House Flanders are buried in a rain of desert sand but emerge victorious. When the dust clears, twenty insurgents are dead, two coalition forces injured, and Camp Fallujah's primary source of water remains secure. SGT David Olson and Specialists Klimek, Knetter, and John Olson earn the Bronze Star Medal with Valor.

In the aftermath of the assault on Pump House Flanders, major security enhancements were added, including a twenty-foot-high bulletproof shield spanning the entire area around the two concrete towers. The shield provided a secondary wall within the tall metal and razor-wire perimeter fence. With the tower shield in place, an elevated walkway was installed between the towers to enable easy, safe access between the towers. The secure living quarters at Flanders became more than a water pumping station—it was a Forward Combat Outpost where we began running patrols into neighboring villages.

At Flanders we worked two- or four-hour shifts; with the longer shifts came more free time. Although Flanders was fairly comfortable, it consisted only of quarters for six troops in the lower level of each tower, three pumps, storage for plenty of food and ammunition, and a relatively safe area between the towers where we ate, lounged, and worked out. Other than watching DVD movies in our rooms, we spent hours working out in a make-shift gymnasium—we got so pumped up, some guys back at Fallujah thought we were taking steroids.

Chapter 15

STARING AN IED IN THE EYES

Hunting insurgents in Iraq is a bit like deer hunting in northern Minnesota, except that back home the animals don't shoot back. When all the birds suddenly go silent and the rabbits and squirrels freeze solid in their tracks you know a predator has invaded their territory. When insurgents lurk about suddenly, there are no cigarette butts on the ground because frightened farmers who love to smoke know they might be killed for smoking and everyone disappears from view. Insurgents don't hesitate to severely beat very young children just for smiling at an American. Insurgents behead the adults or just savagely torture them as an example never to speak with Americans. Villagers claim to hate the insurgents more than we do, but fear is a powerful leash.

They respect our overwhelming power, but they don't fear us in the way they do the insurgents. "Americans are too nice," one village elder says. It's the ultimate good news, bad news conundrum. If we are to succeed in Iraq we need to drive out the insurgents, protect the civilians, work to win their trust, and teach them to defend themselves.

Nelly is on leave in Minnesota; so, SGT Jay Horn is Squad Leader on September 3 and today's patrol is as routine as any. It's the same route we have taken every day for the past week; although today we have two Civil Affairs vehicles tagging along, no big deal. At the first village the Civil Affairs guys drop off school supplies and check to make sure the $10,000 they gave a local sheikh last month for the village's water purification system was not stuffed into his pocket.

They want to change our route to escort engineers into the south area of operation. I like a little excitement as much as the next guy, but I am not a fan of IEDs and that area is infested with them. SSG Kelly Jones' squad hit a big one a couple of days ago. Luckily they were okay, but everyone knows our incredible good luck has to run out sooner or later, hopefully much later. I especially do not like heading into an area we have not scouted, but orders are orders.

I confirm the change order, plot our course, and update my gunner Marine LCpl. Bruce Miller and driver SPC Mark Hoiland on the seriousness of this AO, stressing the need to maintain keen vigilance for anything suspicious. Hoiland, who normally works in the Ground Operations Center—Bravo X-Ray, is getting some experience outside the wire. I don't care if it's a crazed goat. I emphasize *ANYTHING* suspicious. McDonough and Horn are commanding the other two vehicles and giving the same instructions to their crews. Actually, everyone knows what to do; it just feels better talking about it much like a parent might do when handing the car keys to a teenager.

We make the switch, cross over Route Mobile, and stop at Pump House Flanders to repair their radio before easing onto Route Monterey, the IED-infested area south of Flanders. Every eye is fixated on the road for wires, dirt mounds, hoses, or anything that looks sketchy or out of place. I pride myself in being the lead vehicle for the squad, the navigator; but this part of the job still rattles my nerves.

We arrive at the blacktop portion of the road, which is only slightly safer because it is difficult for the insurgents to bury IEDs under blacktop without leaving obvious signs. On blacktop roads they often resort to setting them up on the side of the road, but that will inflict less damage because the explosion is not directly underneath a vehicle.

STARING AN IED IN THE EYES

We keep driving and eventually reach the bridge, aka Checkpoint 32. It's here that Civil Affairs needs to go so we crawl across the bridge alert for hostile activity. Immediately across the bridge, the road takes a sharp left turn, the perfect spot to plant an IED for unsuspecting vehicles rounding the bend. Vigilance pays off as we catch a glimpse of a dubious dirt mound forty meters ahead on the left side of the road. Almost simultaneously, Specialist Hoiland spots the dirt mound and stops abruptly.

No obvious wires are sticking out of the mound; so, I carefully step out of my vehicle to examine the site through my high power scope. Still no wires. Inching ahead on a tightrope, nothing is apparent until I am inexplicably distracted by something much closer. Instant terror grabs my leg in mid-step and every muscle in my body locks tighter than a bronze statue. Staring up at me is another dirt mound less than two feet away inviting my next step with the tip of a mortar round glaring menacingly like a coiled snake, an obvious IED.

Paralysis slaps me with the force of an ocean wave as I expect to be blown apart, but my training instincts kick in as I very slowly ease backward into my own tracks, turn, and run faster than the speed of light, waving my hands and screaming warning to the others. Hoiland slams the Humvee in reverse and tears backward.

Horn shouts into the radio, "Back the fucking trucks up, IED, IED!"

I race right past my vehicle, dive behind Horn's, and take a moment to thank God that I am still alive. My hands are shaking uncontrollably, and I feel every thunderous beat of my heart. I swear it's a jackhammer pounding on concrete and wonder if the guys can hear it. God, are they as terrified as I am? It's said that you never feel more alive than when you have almost died—what they say is absolutely true.

The IEDs that other squads hit on the same road have ripped oversized, heavy-duty tires from giant military vehicles and tossed them one hundred meters like feathers, shattered four-inch thick bullet-proof glass, and crushed heavy armor. To realize how close I just came to becoming nothing more than fragments of bloody, shredded flesh and splintered bone is terrifying.

Explosive Ordinance Disposal (EOD) arrives forty-five minutes later and detonates the bomb, saying that it was a good find, although I'm not so certain the word *good* would be my first choice. On closer inspection EOD discovers that the bomb was a decoy and they tell us the insurgents probably were watching the entire incident perhaps even videotaping it to learn how we react—a realistic training exercise for both sides. Best of all, Bravo Company's incredible good luck remains intact.

Change is the whole theory behind the driving force of combat. If you change, they change to one up you, and then you change again, and it goes on and on leap-frogging forever as it has since cavemen tossed rocks in the first human battle. Of course, there will be mistakes, but errors are amazingly few, thanks to our training, even when you consider the conditions, the risks, the peril, and the tragic consequences of indecision.

We're acquiring plenty of battlefield expertise after three months of kicking down doors, exterminating insurgent rats, and clearing the area surrounding Camp Fallujah to the point that Bravo Company is looked upon much differently by the Marines, especially Colonel Bristol who told embedded journalist Eric Bowen:

Some units are made to fight. These men are the very fiber of what the citizen soldier is all about. This is as fine a company as exists in the military today. At the beginning I don't think they even knew how good they were. The only way you can learn is to go out and to experience with your mind, muscle, bone, blood, and the heart that pumps it; and that's what they have done.

Simply put they are a company of heroes. My wish for them is that they finish their tour strong and that I will see them again in the heartland of America that will seem so much more to them now because they've protected it. The unit that I command is nicknamed the 'Sentinels.' We say that people sleep safe because the Sentinels stand guard. There are no more heroic sentinels than the men of Bravo Company, 2–136th Infantry. They're the finest thing that America produces, and I'm proud to have led them, served with them, and bled with them.

Chapter 16

A Good Day Goes Very Bad

December 2006

We set out on routine patrol December 1, stopping at Pump House Flanders before dawn, where we park our vehicles and hike three miles in full battle gear, taking up positions in the tall weeds and grass, at least what they call grass, along the canal to watch for vehicles planting IEDs. Memories surge back to those days, hiding in backyards at home as we camouflage ourselves by attaching leaves and branches to our helmets. We monitor and record every passing vehicle, but the only action today is a few local farmers tending their sheep and fields, probably laughing at the Americans running through the tall grass with branches stuck on their heads.

The next day we're out early on foot patrol. It's a pretty good day by Iraq standards, a tad cool but in this hell hole cool is always welcome. By noon nothing shows, and we walk back to Flanders for chow and a nap.

1st Lt. Wade Blomgren announces, "There's a report of suspicious activity in a village to our south. Who can go?" Nelly, McDonough, Miller, Rystad, and I jump up heading to our Humvee, and Everson,

My best camouflage act lying in wait for insurgents

Rystad checks out the Euphrates

McDonough and I try to blend into background watching for insurgents planting IEDs

McDonough and Rystad lying in the tall grass on patrol December 1

Gallant, and Seed climb into their Bradley Fighting Vehicle. I feel like commanding the vehicle today, so I take the front seat with McDonough as my driver, Nelson gets in behind me, Rystad is behind McDonough, and Miller moves into the gunner's hatch.

Approaching the area, I spot a teenage boy who glances back at us like somebody who just ripped off a six-pack from the corner store. As we draw near, he bolts and vanishes into a house.

"Stop, let's check this out," I say. While Miller covers us with the machine gun, we enter the house with guns ready as we have done dozens of times before. We know that we are a terrifying sight busting through the door of the crude mud house; but surprise and overwhelming force is the safest approach for us and, strangely, for the occupants who generally cooperate instantly, avoiding the need for a more aggressive response.

There's no easy way to tell the bad guys from the ordinary citizens. I won't call any of them good guys because I don't see many who are truly blameless. Even those who aren't overtly attacking us are complicit in some way if only by their silence. They never get blown away by the scores of IEDs planted throughout their neighborhood because they know where the bombs are planted.

"Bravo One, this is Bravo Six, come back," Lieutenant Blomgren calls.

"Bravo One," Seed replies.

"Bravo One, check for suspicious activity in the area of Checkpoint 34."

"Roger, suspicious activity at Checkpoint 34."

We jump back in our vehicles and head down the road passing Checkpoint 32 about two miles from camp in a desolate open area along the canal that leads from the Euphrates River to Pump House Barney. We're searching for anything that could be an IED, creeping cautiously at five to ten miles an hour. McDonough is doing his best to stay in the tracks of the Bradley to avoid setting off an IED, or, as the news guys say, "roadside bomb."

In this area most of the roads are little more than dirt paths, a few have some gravel. Insurgents love unpaved roads so they can bury their bombs in the center for maximum damage. Their favored trigger system is a pressure plate or victim operated IED. I hate the term "victim operated"; it almost sounds like the victim has a choice. He doesn't.

We try to have the same teams travel regularly through the same areas so they can detect even the slightest irregularity; often, that indicates a new bomb. Our lives may depend on spotting the simple signs set out to warn locals about bomb locations, something as subtle as a brick turned at a different angle, a pop bottle on the ground where there had been none yesterday, or a dead animal.

Everson and Gallant are two of the very best we have at spotting IEDs, a unique skill that can mean the difference between life and death. "Situational awareness" is the key stressed by Everson over and over. The high powered 15x magnified scanner aboard their Bradleys is also very helpful. He defines "situational awareness" as common sense amplified one hundred times. Stay alert to your surroundings. Record every minute detail in your head. If you look around and there are no goats or children, and gardens and yards are empty, assume something is wrong—the locals know when to hide, what roads to avoid, and they never hit the bombs.

In the farmlands surrounding Camp Fallujah, foreign terrorists are rarely seen because they stand out in the sparsely populated region. They dwell mostly in the large cities, sneaking around in nondescript small trucks. In the rural areas, they pay impoverished farmers to dig holes in specific locations and then arrive to plant their bombs and race away as rapidly as possible. They cut a large hole in the bed of their truck to enable one rat to crawl down the hole beneath the truck while a second person walks alongside and takes a leak to distract any observers, trying his best to look casual. In moments the bomb is in place and the hole is covered ready for an unsuspecting American to pass over it.

I call in Checkpoint 33 as we search for anything out of place. We turn a corner, following one hundred meters behind the Bradley, and the world goes upside down. The blast actually doesn't sound that loud to me, or perhaps it's just so loud that it's quiet, if that makes any sense. It is like when you jump into a pool and sound is muted, or that ringing you hear an hour or two after leaving a super-loud concert. Then comes the unforgettable sound of small rocks raining down on metal, and feeling myself in a twisted, uncomfortable pile on the ground. I don't remember flying through the air, but I'm definitely aware of what's going on as I lie on the ground, praying that I will live long enough for the medevac helicopter to arrive. I know my chance of surviving is not good. I don't feel much pain, but I'm scared.

It's weird what goes through your head. I'm thinking how we are—make that *were*—the only squad never to hit an IED, and nobody in Bravo Company has been seriously injured. I guess our incredible good luck just ran out.

Taking a few minutes before our last patrol
December 2, two hours before the explosion. Shown from
left to right are LCpl. Bruce Miller, SSG Tim Nelson, SPC
Bryan McDonough, me, and SPC Corey Rystad

Front view of our Humvee sitting in the scrap yard with the engine, windshield, and gunners turret ripped away

Our Humvee on the road after it was tipped back to the left shortly after the explosion. I landed just to the right with the vehicle hovering over me

Chapter 17

EIGHT DAYS LOST IN A COMA

I lost eight days in December 2006, but I didn't lose my life thanks to an incredible confluence of guardian angels who walked with me in the desert dust northeast of Fallujah and through each step from the CSH (Combat Surgical Hospital) at Al-Taqaddum Air Base; the critical care center at Balad Air Base near Baghdad; the surgical center at Landstuhl Regional Medical Center in Frankfurt, Germany; and Walter Reed Army Medical Center in Washington, D.C.

Because I was not conscious for eight days after the IED blast, those who were at my side will tell that part of the story:

Captain Charles "Chip" Rankin, commander, Bravo Company, 2–136th Infantry

I just happened to be attending a conference at Al-Taqaddum Air Base (better known as TQ) when the battalion commander, Lieutenant Colonel Gregg Parks, pulls me aside and reveals that a Humvee from 1st Platoon, Bravo Company, was just blown up by an IED and the casualties are headed to TQ. First reports say that SPC Bryan McDonough was killed and the other four are injured, at least

CPT Rankin visits me at Walter Reed during a tour home. He drove several hours to visit and take me to Ruby Tuesdays.

two seriously. In the battlefield first reports are always wrong.

There are so many ifs and maybes that you could go insane rethinking decisions. I guess that happens every time there is a tragedy, and I have done plenty of it myself. On December 2 we received a report of suspicious activity and relayed the information to the nearest units at Pump House Flanders. Several of my guys were on a two-day patrol and were at Flanders when the message came through.

McDonough, normally the gunner, decided to drive and Bruce Miller, the only Marine in the group, moved from driver to gunner. Kriesel assumed vehicle command and climbed into the front right seat as squad leader; normally Tim Nelson would have been there and Kriesel would have been in a different vehicle.

The Bradley, a much heavier, highly armored vehicle that is a small tank, led the way. To minimize risk of striking an IED, every vehicle in the patrol follows track in track. Unfortunately, the Bradley wheelbase is slightly wider than the Humvee. (Investigators later determine that the Bradley missed the IED by as little as two or three inches, that difference in wheelbase width meant the Humvee was on a slightly different track, directly over the IED.) Up to that point most of the IEDs we encountered used twenty to fifty pounds of explosive, but the insurgents apparently were targeting a Bradley with this 200-pound bomb.

The TQ medical facility is the primary trauma center serving all of Western Iraq and is staffed by highly experienced Marine and Navy emergency doctors; fortunately for Kriesel it is only a short helicopter ride from the incident site.

The bird lands and John is the first one out. One of his legs, still attached by a thread of skin and a few strands of fabric from his uniform pants, is flopped up on his torso like a piece of extra equipment, and the other leg is just a bloody stump. He is totally out of it with his arms dragging like limp ropes; he's an extreme mess.

Medics race him into surgery where surgeons and nurses are waiting. John dies three times on the surgery table, and each time they shock him back to life, but nobody really expects him to survive. They just don't give up without a fight as long as there's any sign of life.

Bruce Miller comes next. He doesn't have any visible injuries but is pretty incoherent. Tim Nelson is close behind followed by the body that I assume is McDonough. We discover that Miller suffered a serious concussion.

Nelson comes right up to me and pummels me with questions, "What happened? What's going on? How are my guys?" Immediately I realize he might have a head injury as well. His memory is about ten to fifteen seconds long, and then he starts asking the same questions over and over and over. "How are my guys? How are my guys?"

I don't want to tell him the truth just yet, so I tell him they're going to be okay.

"What happened? How are my guys?"

Initially it appears that Nelson has a broken tailbone, but that isn't the case. All he seems to care about is getting back to Fallujah to be with the rest of his guys because he doesn't want to let them down; but he is in tough shape physically, and emotionally he is having difficulty dealing with the damage to his good friend and roommate, John Kriesel.

One of the medical staff asks if I can come back to identify the soldier who was killed. They uncover the body. It's a disaster, and I don't recognize who it is, but I know for sure that it isn't Bryan McDonough.

"This isn't Bryan."

"We know. It's Corey Rystad."

"Corey?" My mind does somersaults. This is Cory Rystad? I was prepared for Bryan; this can't be Corey, but it is. There's his nametag. I just wasn't prepared for it to be Corey. He wasn't listed in any of the early reports, and suddenly here he is lying in front of me, dead. I had dinner with Corey two nights ago, and we made plans to go bow hunting at Camp Ripley after our tour.

The priest arrives and administers last rites. No amount of training can prepare you for this. I'm numb with shock, but I go with John and Tim as they are moved to the flight line where they board a C-130 for the trip to Balad Air Base, the best medical facility in Iraq.

Once they depart for Balad, I manage to grab a chopper flight back to Camp Fallujah with General Miller where my mission is to find out what happened to McDonough. One of the first people I encounter is Corporal Miller who explains that McDonough died at the scene and was brought back to Fallujah in the QRF ambulance. So much for hope.

The next day is even more difficult for me, if that's possible. I call John's wife, Katie. Through a snafu she had not been officially notified. She got the word from his parents, and she is furious with the Army.

When I call she unloads on me. Wow! That's tough, almost as bad as talking to Rystad's and McDonough's parents. I know she is really hurting; so, I let her get it all out and then I try to give her the no bullshit conversation, honestly telling her everything I know. I call FRG (Family Readiness Group) to get her some assistance for the flight to Landstuhl, Germany, where John is heading, although she already has her travel plans well underway before FRG can react. I am just hoping he survives long enough for her to get there; but everything I am being told indicates he is going to die. Somehow he survives, unquestionably in no small measure due to Katie. She's a remarkable young woman.

I go back to my soldiers, and we figure out how to carry on as we head out on patrol the next day. One thing is certain—Bravo Company's incredible good luck just ran out.

SSG Tim Nelson, best friend and roommate

We are only five minutes out of the village when the blast hits. It isn't really a blast in the sense of a tremendous, deafening roar as much as a subtle "poing" sound similar to what you might expect when a rock strikes the side of an empty fifty-five gallon metal oil drum. I am flying through the air flipping with the ease of an Olympic gymnast, but the landing is more like a motorcycle stunt driver crashing on his jump over a string of cars. I try to get up, but my body isn't obeying my commands. As the dust begins to settle, I sense blood oozing from shrapnel imbedded in my face, but I'm able to lift up enough to survey the scene and it's ugly.

SSG Nelson on guard in main tower at Pump House Flanders

First I spot my roommate Kriesel. John is in a lot of pain, and I can see his legs are nothing but shredded ribbons connected to him only by his Army combat uniform (ACU), the camouflage uniform worn by today's soldiers. Corey Rystad is pinned under the Humvee, and Gallant is working like a crazed man to keep him alive. He forces air into Corey's lungs and with every breath he inhales blood. Gallant looks like a vampire with crimson liquid dripping from his chin as he fights to breathe life into Rystad's shattered body.

I can't move, but I have to help. The only thing I can do is keep yelling at Kriesel. "Hang in there, Kries. Don't give up. You're going to make it." I don't know if it helps or drives him crazy, but I keep at it until the medics load us onto the chopper and then I black out for the next twenty-four hours. Actually, there are brief moments of consciousness almost like a strobe light flashing with eerie film clips aboard the chopper, again at TQ while sliding into the CAT scan machine, and then being lifted from the stretcher onto a bed.

Finally I'm awake and a nurse is standing there holding my wrist, peppering me with questions I don't comprehend or answer. I ask her about Rystad and McDonough. She ignores me, and I start thinking maybe they weren't injured as badly as we were, since they aren't here. Miller is in the bed next to me, but he doesn't have any answers either. I just keep asking the same questions over and over and over about four thousand times. It probably drives him and everyone else crazy, but for some strange reason I can't remember anything more than a few seconds.

Moments later the thought that Corey and Bryan survived is crushed when the sergeant major arrives and explains that they died in the explosion. The realization ignites vivid memories of the blast scene. I can't do a damn thing other than stand in the shower for a long, long time trying to wash away the dirt, the blood, and the memories.

At Balad Air Base, forty miles north of Baghdad, they hold me at the hospital two days for observation and that provides an opportunity to sit with Kriesel in one of the gigantic tents that serve as a hospital. This labyrinth of tents contains eighteen intensive care unit beds, forty intermediate beds, and eight operating-room tables where they treat approximately 3,800 patients every month, with an unprecedented ninety-seven-percent survival rate. Patients include U.S. military, civilians, and contractors; Iraqi military and civilians; and enemy combatants.

John's bed is in the middle of an immense tent, and there I sit next to him on a bar stool. The floor is a mass of wood packing skids put in place with a forklift and covered by a large canvas tarpaulin. Hallways connecting the big tents are unfinished plywood wallpapered with posters, military orders, photographs, and random messages.

This may not be the finest hospital in the world, but it is possibly the busiest, and at the moment, it is the difference between life and death as I talk to John's motionless, shredded body for four or five hours, praying he will make it. I just can't lose another guy.

Finally the doctors are confident that Kries is stable enough to travel. For the trip, they slide him into a gigantic, heated nylon bag known as a "hot pocket," with nothing but a breathing tube visible, and race to the flight line. As they move down the hallway, many people assume the guy in what appears to be a body bag has died, but John is in a fierce battle to live. Miller is also loaded into the aircraft for transfer to Germany.

"Don't worry," Miller says, "I'll take care of him."

At that point, I just want to get the hell out of there, go back to my guys, and destroy the bastards who planted that bomb. This place with its collage of big tents attempting to be a hospital is driving me crazy. The constant rap rap rapping of helicopters coming and going. Nurses racing. Doctors racing. Everybody is running to grab new victims off the choppers all through the day and night and rushing them under the big top. It's quite a circus of organized chaos, and it is about to drive me out of my mind.

Before I can leave, they give me a battery of memory tests. I caution them that my memory was not so good in the first place. They don't laugh, but I must have passed because they send me "home" to Camp Fallujah where life is pure torture without my roommate. In battle you build an insane bond with your brothers; but your roommate is almost part of your very soul, the guy who knows everything about you, your confidant. Here I am with half of my soul ripped away and spirited off to who knows where while I am left to wonder if he is even still alive. Staring at his empty bed, I talk to him and I swear he answers.

I'm getting antsy to get back into the field, but I'm still on medical profile and need Colonel Bristol's permission. After talking with the medics he gives the go ahead, but quickly adds, "You are still banged up a bit. I can't let you go out there as a squad leader, but you can be Captain Rankin's driver."

Hell, that's fine. If that's what it takes to get me outside the wire, I'll be a driver. On my first run with Rankin, we're out about four hours when "phffffft" something whistles right past our faces and slams into a decaying, gray concrete building next to us, leaving a faint trail of smoke across our hood.

Instinctively, I throw the Humvee into reverse, crush the gas pedal, and shoot blindly backward into a ditch, escaping their line of sight just as a second RPG rips through the exact spot where we had been seconds earlier and explodes against the building. I radio in to report the incoming RPG rounds from the village, and two other Humvees arrive quickly to assist us.

We're barely back underway when I spot a red water can lying alongside the road. The lead Humvee has already zipped past it, but at the last second I spot the telltale beads of an IED strung across the road, resembling a string of Christmas lights. I swerve hard left, but our right front tire crushes one of the Christmas lights, igniting a soft pop and a spray of confetti; amazingly only the blasting cap discharges.

"Whoa! Wow!" Rankin and I exhale in unison and stare at each other in shock. We jump from the Humvee, duck into a nearby building and summon the Emergency Ordinance Disposal team once again.

EOD pulls a 155mm African artillery round from the sand that would have destroyed our Humvee. "God, have I become a bomb magnet?" I mumble to myself.

A few days later we're back at the site of the December 2 blast, examining the mammoth crater. It's four to five feet deep and eight-feet across, but pictures can't capture the magnitude in actual size or the emotion of what happened here. I grab a couple pieces of shrapnel, one for me and one for Kriesel.

The EOD team arrives once more with their high-tech vehicles to sweep the area and on the first run they pull eight IEDs out of the road that we have been traveling every day. The scumbags were just waiting for the right moment to activate the bombs as they have been doing throughout October and November. IEDs are exploding continuously, and each time we hear another one we can only pray that no one is injured. By some miracle, nobody was seriously injured until December 2.

We always knew the threat was real, but somehow we seemed to be living under a shroud of protection. Life in a battle zone is always grim, but after the blast everything grew dark, more ominous.

After December 2, Army life at Camp Fallujah shifted to a much higher gear. COL George Bristol went out on foot patrols more often and in vehicles with us. He saw with his own eyes what needed to be done and gave orders to act. Before Bristol our commanders were satisfied to sit behind their desks, issuing orders without soiling their neatly pressed uniforms.

If there is anything positive, our leaders finally begin to take a serious interest in all the suspicious activity we have been reporting for months. Suddenly we are doing full company and even a few full battalion missions into villages. SPC Brian Micheletti and a couple of Marines are assigned to my squad to replace the guys we lost as we push the circle of protection farther and farther south into known insurgent strongholds going door to door. Headquarters sends down a new BOLO list of wanted insurgents believed to be in our area of operations.

Shortly after Christmas we launch Operation Sledgehammer, a full company raid into an area on the Euphrates River twenty kilometers south of Fallujah that had been out of our normal patrol area, giving the insurgents a false sense of security. In fact, the area around the village of Zaidon has become a virtual safe haven for insurgents to the point that we catch them by surprise.

Each squad gets a short list of houses to search, and we launch simultaneous raids before they can awaken to sound the alarm. We hit the first one busting through the door at 0300 hours while everybody is asleep. Maurstad grabs one guy in the first room who is fumbling around for a pistol hidden under his pillow; he's on the

BOLO list of known terrorists. I take the room on the right and pick off another BOLO guy who is sound asleep next to his wife. In the third room, Micheletti arrests an old guy, apparently father of the other two, who is also on the BOLO list. Later, Brian endures some teasing for taking down a senior citizen.

With the three guys handcuffed, we search the house and find a huge cache of weapons, including numerous pistols, eight AK-47s, boxes of grenades and more than $1,000 in U.S. currency, a pretty unusual find. Iraqis are allowed to have one weapon per household for protection, usually an AK-47, but no long-range rifles or anything with a scope. This is way over the top.

Simultaneously, Second Platoon hits a house just south of our position and uncovers a "torture house" where two Iraqi victims are imprisoned. From the outside, it's an ordinary single-story stucco and mud house with typical dirt floors, blending into the neighborhood. The only doors on Iraqi houses are the entry doors, once inside there are no doors, merely archways separating rooms. Occasionally a curtain conceals a bedroom.

Inside this house is far from ordinary. The two victims are lying on rusty old beds with only metal springs, no mattress or sheets where they have been systematically tortured by insurgents who are nowhere to be found. The insurgent objective here was not so much information gathering as it was sending a strong message to any village that cooperates with the Americans. Victims generally are village leaders or children of leaders.

Lead pipes are used to break bones in the arms and legs, and the insurgents are careful to avoid killing victims too quickly. Battered victims are dumped back into the village sometimes barely alive, but frequently they are dead by the time they are found. In either case, the message is clear—don't talk to the Americans. Next to the beds we find wires plugged into an outlet for use in administering electroshock treatments to the victims, usually on the genitals.

The room is decorated in dark, dried blood splatter and bloody handprints are everywhere reminding me of something much darker than the handprint art a kindergartener might bring home from school. Nobody is living in this place; in fact, the only residents at the moment are the two victims who are unable to move let alone escape. One guy has virtually every bone in both arms and legs broken, and we send him out by medevac helicopter. In time he will recover. The other guy, son of the local village leader, has not been here long and has only minor injuries. We take him home to a grateful family.

We uncover another major cache of weapons, grenades, and a truckload of propane tanks with the bottoms cut off to build IEDs, identical to the two that blew up our Humvee on December 2. The propane tanks are squirreled away in a dented, dirty, blue bongo truck ready for loading with explosives and planting in roads along our routes. The place also contains a virtual Goodwill shop of clothing, police uniforms, and disguises.

We fill the torture house with C4 explosives and level it in a spectacular blast—a different sort of message for the villagers.

Okay, we're finally starting to find out where these scumbags are hiding, making bombs, and terrorizing the villagers. We arrest eighteen of them, some Saudis and a few Iraqis. Many of the serious insurgents are from outside the area, often not Iraqis. They provide the weapons, bombs, and money and intimidate the locals to carry out their dirty work.

A couple weeks later, we launch another massive mission into the area, but this time there is no element of surprise. Following the last mission, insurgents started planting IEDs in their own neighborhood; so, we need an EOD team to lead the way. They uncover seven armed IEDs in our path. They clear the bombs, but the process impedes rapid assault and sounds the alarm giving the rats time to slither down their holes. We never have the success of the first raid again, but we keep pushing the scumbags farther and farther away from Fallujah and things improve markedly. Our battle space is almost void of IEDs; mortar attacks become rare, and we begin to drive through the area in relative safety. Best of all, the villagers relax and become more confident and cooperative.

We are doing EOD sweeps every two days and conducting intense searches of the villages. The violence has almost stopped. One can only wonder what took so long for our leaders to act. At the squad level, we just carry out our missions and send in reports. Man, do we send in reports. At times it seems that we spend more time writing reports than fighting. I wonder if the insurgents ever have to do paperwork.

A month after Bryan and Cory died, and John was blown apart, Jimmy Wosika is killed less than a kilometer from our blast site. If life was dark and ominous after December 2, it is downright hopeless on January 9, 2007, when Jimmy dies. The very next day we get news that we are being extended four months. Hopeless turns to despair and mass depression. Morale can't get any lower, but, as squad leader, it's my job to put a positive spin on life and keep my little brothers motivated. *Right.*

We are convinced that Bravo Company has already carried most of the load for the whole battalion, and we're more than ready to depart Camp Fallujah when orders come telling us to fall back to TQ. Amazingly, on arrival we're treated like outcasts; maybe it's jealousy or embarrassment from riding our coattails.

Being at TQ doesn't change a thing other than being in an even crappier camp and saddled with more leaders giving orders. We are sent out on even more patrols stretching farther and farther into the northern reaches of Anbar Province. Another company has the misfortune to hit an IED killing one of their guys, and they refuse to go out again—we didn't realize that was an option. We end up pulling their shift, too; whoever said life isn't fair definitely got it right.

The only good thing about TQ is that I am able to go to ECP #2 (Commander's Post) with Captain Rankin and call Kriesel at Walter Reed. We talk for an hour the first time, and it makes things a lot better for all of us. It is one less worry, and he gives us something positive to talk about. We are ecstatic when John tells us how well he is being treated, and he reassures us that the Army has our backs. Wow, if he can be that positive, so can we.

SFC Rene Montero, friend since Kosovo

We had a rough day at work.

"Kriesel got hit and he's pretty messed up," SGT Seth Steinbach explodes into my room clutching the casualty report. In short, two KIA (killed in action) and three WIA (wounded in action). The wounded are being brought to Balad CSH (Combat Surgical Hospital), the largest medical facility in Iraq, where Steinbach and I are stationed.

Once they arrive, I'm standing in the hospital intensive care unit and the nurses are talking to me but I don't hear them. My gear is heavy; I'm dirty and I'm tired. None of that matters because I'm looking at what's left of my friend. It's devastating to see him this way.

Kriesel survived an IED blast, but two of his Joes didn't make it. I recognize his swollen face and the tattoos, but not much else. He has multiple tubes and wires running from him. He's in a medically induced coma, and machines are keeping him alive. An electrocardiogram (EKG) is beeping rhythmically, and the respirator chugs along as it breathes for him. An electroencephalograph (EEG) shows brain activity, but there's no telling how much damage has been done.

SFC Rene Montero

His eyes are taped shut because of swelling; he has a gastro-intestinal tube in his nose and an intubation tube (breathing tube) down his throat. His left arm is cut open and wet-packed with bandages to allow the tissue to safely swell and return to normal without additional tissue damage. His stomach and pelvis are wet-packed for the same reason, and a drain tube has been installed to stave off infection from the surgery he has survived. His right leg has been amputated below the knee and his left leg just above the knee. So far, he's had three surgeries to stabilize him for transport to Germany. The nurses tell me he's had almost all of his blood replaced with donated blood, but they are not sure if he will survive.

"It's up to him, now," one says.

Here's a soldier who I've been in charge of for a number of years. I, and my fellow sergeants, groomed and mentored him for leadership and taught him everything we could. At the start of this deployment, there was nothing more we could teach him that he couldn't learn on his own. He always led by example, took care of his Joes, and made the mission happen.

As a friend, John was like having a stand-up comedian with you 24/7, an exceedingly intelligent comedian, at that. He would do anything for any of us if we needed him to, from helping us with computer problems (yes, grunts are smart) to just going out and having a few beers. You could always count on Kries, especially when we needed a boost in spirit.

Patrolling in Iraq is just a matter of pushing your luck. Our equipment is second to none; the training can't be matched, and the Army works incessantly to ensure our safety. But it all truly boils down to pushing your luck. Kriesel's luck ran out, and his Humvee got hit. That's just the way it is in a war zone. You can be a total dirt bag; you go out in sector every day, and you leave here without a scratch. Or, you can be God's gift to the Army, a super stud, and you get smoked on your first hour in sector. It's just the nature of this place. There's no sense to it, no justice, no fairness. War will test anyone's faith.

As I'm standing in the ICU covered with dirt, blood, and four-day-old stench, I realize that angels truly are among us. Some just happen to be wearing surgical gowns and fatigues. They just bring my soldier out of surgery and are talking to him as they are going about their business, never mind that he can't hear a word they say. These angels are taking care of other wounded warriors, catching up on paperwork, and involving the wounded in their conversations as if they were part of the family.

Kries was a bit of a "player" when he was single, but came to the point when he wanted to settle down, get married, and have a family. God worked his magic and placed Katie and John in each other's lives at a crucial time. Now I start to think about what is going to happen to Katie and their two little boys.

Kriesel is totally unconscious, but I pull up a chair and start talking to him, "catching up" with recent events such as home, family, football, deployment, rumors, and the like. I laugh out loud recalling some of the funny things that happened to us on previous deployments, bad things we suffered through, and plans for when we get home. It doesn't seem unusual or out of place for me to do so. The medics have already spun me up on all the damage; so, I know what to expect. But, it is still unnerving to see it happen to a person you've known for so long. I tell him how things are here in Balad compared to where he's been stationed in Fallujah, and I complain about work. I am there for almost two hours catching up in a one-way conversation.

I pray for him, but not in the manner that one might expect. I ask God that if Kries is not going to survive, please take him now while he's sleeping and at peace. If it's time for him to die, let it be now so that Katie and the boys don't have to see him like this, broken, shredded, and torn.

The ICU area where Kries is being treated is known as "the gate" because most of the guys who arrive here are at the gateway between life and death. In preparation for this journey, visiting soldiers normally place coins and money on the cots next to the wounded soldiers to pay Kharon the ferryman. According to Greek mythology, Kharon took the newly dead across the River Styx if they could pay the fare. Those who could not pay or those whose bodies were left unburied had to wander the banks of the river for one hundred years. Coins to pay Kharon for passage were placed on the tombstone, on the eyes, or in the mouth of the dead person in order for them to pay atonement for their sins in life. This tradition has become a ritual among soldiers, sailors, airmen, and marines. Many of us are not exactly saints during our lives, especially in combat; but we do have a tremendous amount of empathy and camaraderie toward one another.

I take a break just to get away for a few minutes, to store my gear, and to grab a quick bite to eat. When I return, several coins already have been placed on his cot, just in case. In the war zone, there are not real beds, just cots; so, they use wool blankets or whatever is available to comfort patients on top of cots or litters, making it easier to transport patients quickly to and from locations and aircraft. Kriesel is on a litter so that he is ready for immediate transport when the time comes. The first thing I notice is the litter next to Kriesel is now empty. The nurses tell me that guy died a few minutes ago. There he was right next to me, and I never even knew his name.

Steinbach arrives. Neither of us is certain how long we have been awake, but it doesn't matter. The only thing that exists right now is that Kries is with his brothers. The nurses return with news that they need to get him ready for transport to the regional medical center in Germany.

Steinbach and I take off our combat patches, write our names on them with a black felt-tip pen, and tape them and a brief note to Kries so if he wakes up he knows he was with his brothers and never alone. We say a quick prayer and kiss his forehead good-bye.

One of the nurses finds all this unusual and asks me about it. Apparently most visitors are too rattled to say anything significant to the wounded. I tell her that I was just spending time with my friend whom I haven't seen in a little while. Whether it's here or back home, he's still my friend. I'll be there for him and his family. The patch thing is because I don't have anything else of value on me to tell him I was there. He'll understand when he comes out of sedation. It's easy to forget the important things in our lives and to allow situations to overwhelm our priorities, so we don't. Kriesel just needs to know, we've got his back.

Steinbach and I go back to war. We don't stop thinking about Kries and his family; it's just what soldiers do.

ART FLOURISHES, EVEN IN A WAR ZONE

SFC Rene Montero is a gifted artist who painted cartoons for Disney between military enlistments, and he used his skill to build rapport with Iraqi citizens in Balad. The people were so impressed with the giant, patriotic mural he created on two 20-ton sections of a "T-wall," constructed to deflect rockets and mortar shrapnel, that there was a constant procession of citizens asking to have their photograph taken with Sergeant Montero. The mural included a panel titled "In Honor Of" listing those who died, and Montero dutifully performed the grim task of updating his work. He also posted a panel explaining "Why We're Here" with dates and death tolls of major insurgent attacks leading up to the war:

October 23, 1983	Marine Barracks, Beirut, Lebanon	243
December 21, 1988	PanAm Flight 103, Lockerbie, Scotland	244
February 26, 1993	World Trade Center, New York City	6
June 25, 1995	Khobar towers, Dhahran, Saudi Arabia	19
August 7, 1998	U.S. Embassies in Kenya and Tanzania	224
October 12, 2000	USS Cole, Aden, Yemen	17
September 11, 2001	World Trade Center, New York City	2,819
	United Airlines Flight 93	40
	U.S. Pentagon, Washington, D.C.	125

Montero's patriotic wall painting

Intricate design urn made by Iraqi artist from scrounged brass bullet casings

Painting with frame of camel bone, dyed reeds and brass from shell casings

Although we didn't see a great deal of artistic expression in the rural areas outside of Fallujah (Balad and Baghdad) where Montero was stationed had a much deeper history in the fine arts. In fact, deposed dictator Sadam Hussein encouraged artists; although, the subject matter of their pursuit was limited to paintings and sculptures of Hussein.

Even in the midst of war, artistic people find a way to express their talent. With money and art materials in short supply, they scoured battlefields scooping up empty brass shell casings and melted the brass into wooden or concrete molds. Once removed from the molds, the small sculptures were coated with auto paint. Next a paper stencil with a hand-drawn design was attached to the brass "blank." The artist then carefully etched the pattern. The process took anywhere from a few days to several months.

Two-dimensional paintings also flourished in the Iraqi art community, but the picture frames into which the art was placed often were even more detailed and spectacular than the paintings. Picture frames were enhanced with camel bone, tinted reeds, and reclaimed brass. Reeds were first dyed to the desired color. Then bone and reeds were cut to various geometrical shapes and combined with brass to complete an intricate pattern and embedded into the wooden frame using a cutting cable. The actual painting generally was produced on thin slices of camel rib bones. A single painting took one to ten months.

SGT Todd Everson, friend

Back at Camp Fallujah, we clean up Bryan's, Corey's, and John's gear for return to their families. In the midst of cleanup, the brigade commander, COL David Elicerio, calls me on the phone and starts asking all kinds of questions. When I realize his concern isn't about our guys as much as it is about creating an instructional video, I start to boil. He's dissecting our mission, asking over and over, "What would you have done differently? How could you not see that?" That lights my fuse, and I'm about to rip into a full colonel. Luckily we aren't face to face because I probably would have decked him.

SGT Todd Everson

CPT Chip Rankin, our company commander, rips the phone from my hand, asks the colonel to stand by, and punches the hold button just in time to save my career. "You don't need to listen to this right now," he says and waves me out of the room. "I'll take it from here. I have sworn statements from everyone; that's all he needs for now."

The truth is, I wouldn't have done anything differently, but the insurgents are getting pretty damn good at planting big bombs. I'm convinced that our Bradley was their real target with that two hundred-pound bomb. If they could destroy a Bradley tank, they would be sending a strong message. Unfortunately, an up-armored Humvee is no match for a gigantic bomb designed to destroy a tank.

Our National Guard company at Camp Fallujah often found more than fifty IEDs a day. Gallant and I found fifty-eight in one day ourselves. Marine Commander COL George Bristol addressed us just before we left Iraq and applauded the job we had done finding almost 1,500 IEDs.

I hit an IED with the Bradley one day and blew off the track. We were sitting ducks out in the field for three hours, scanning with our weapons to fend off insurgent attacks; fortunately none showed. Once the track was repaired, we headed back to camp and, on the way, we discovered fifteen more IEDs, seven of which we had already passed over; but luckily they weren't activated. My driver had a sore back, but otherwise we suffered no serious injuries. Gallant came racing out to back us up, and he, too, ran over all the IEDs without incident. The insurgents are getting so good at planting IEDs that it is becoming more and more difficult to spot the bombs even with our high-tech scanning devices and experience.

Intensity ratchets up about fifteen notches after December 2 as Colonel Bristol sends us out to get some answers, focusing along the Euphrates River area south of Fallujah where Rystad, McDonough, and Kriesel were hit. We move into Zaidon, the village nearest the explosion site, as well as several other neighboring villages. Calling these places villages is a bit misleading; they aren't really towns in the sense of having commercial districts. They are merely residential settlements, small clusters of shabby mud and cement shacks, where farmers live in groups.

It's almost embarrassing when we can't stop thinking about what happened here, but we ease cautiously down the same roads almost being timid, especially in the area where the guys were hit. Your breath tightens up, and we get light-headed just thinking about traveling down the same road, a road we traveled many times before December 2. One major shift in thinking is how we react to IED reports. Before the explosion, we had plenty of blasts, but usually no one was injured or the injuries were minor. That all changed December 2. Now any time there is an incident, we freeze in fearful anticipation until we hear the report.

On the road back to Fallujah one day after Christmas, we are passing the village and start taking small arms fire. A couple of rocket-propelled grenades rip past, exploding harmlessly in the desert. RPGs keep getting closer, zeroing in on our position. We realize the insurgents are firing from the safety of a nearby school and call Bravo X-ray at Fallujah for artillery support. A minute later the school vanishes in a cloud of dust. Thankfully, there are no students present, although this is definitely a teaching moment for the entire village.

Nothing much unusual is found until I spot one of our M16 rifles resting against the wall in a farmhouse. We grab the guy and haul him back to Pump House Flanders. As tempting as it is, we refrain from physical abuse; the moron may have just found it or bought it. We aren't able to get any information from him; so, we send him back to Camp Fallujah, where trained Marine interrogators take over. If he knows anything, they will extract the information.

Katie, my wonderful wife

A piercing, intermittent shriek jerks me awake shortly after midnight Sunday, December 3, and I know without answering that

the phone is screaming bad news about John.

"Katie, you need to sit up," John's mother says.

"Oh, God, tell me he's not dead!"

"Katie, he's alive; but it's really bad."

Somehow I manage to call my mother who lives less than a mile away. Instantly, she recognizes something is very wrong even if she can't decipher my anguished stammer. Racing to our house, she fears something has happened to Broden or Elijah.

Katie Kriesel relaxing in the chair in Room 5735 that was her bed for eight months

I lie awake on the couch waiting and worrying until seven a.m. when I start calling around trying to get more information on where John is and how he is doing. I'm barely conscious of anything as I stumble about the house, trying to maintain some sense of normalcy for the boys, even taking them to breakfast at the Cottage Grove VFW Sunday morning to see Santa Claus.

After breakfast I call Nancy Matthews, my friend and boss at Eagle Global Logistics (EGL). Nancy quickly notifies another Eagle staffer and mutual friend, Jennifer Sawicki, who lives nearby in Cottage Grove. Jen arrives within minutes, and Nancy is not far behind. My mom takes on the task of notifying other family members and close friends.

The boys know something is up. I fight to keep my voice even and hold back the tears, but they know something is very, very wrong. I send them off to their hockey game with Grandma and Papa while I continue to wait for news, and wait, and wait. Sunday feels like a week as I wait in agony for news, dreading that it is going to be bad.

Finally, word comes that John is on his way to Germany. Now I need to figure out how to get there. I don't even have a passport, only my military ID, but my employer is in the international transportation and logistics business, and that proves to be an enormous asset.

We go to the computer where Nancy starts pulling information off the Internet for my passport application and flight options. She Googles Landstuhl, Germany. Once we figure out how to spell it, she discovers what options are for accommodations. I get on the phone and track down the doctor assigned to John's case at Landstuhl Regional Medical Center. He cautions me to hold off; John has not even arrived in Germany yet, but he is in the air.

The head surgeon explains, "Normally people only stay here twenty-four hours. We'll just stabilize him and get him to the United States as fast as possible because his chance of survival will increase dramatically once he gets to the United States. I don't want you to come here and pass him on the way."

The boys return from hockey and need dinner, thank goodness

the Carlson's, friends from my small group Bible study at church, dropped off food because I don't think I could figure out how to boil water at this point. I sit silently at the table with the boys while they eat, and they both stare into my red eyes, and I realize it's time to tell them something. I just don't know what to tell them. I want to say he is going to be fine, but I know that is not a good idea, in case he dies. At this point, I don't know what is going to happen. "Daddy got hurt really bad, and Mommy might need to go help him at the hospital far away in a place called Germany"

"What kind of hurt?" Elijah asks.

"Dad doesn't have legs anymore."

They go silent as they absorb the news, a giant burden for little guys, now four and five "and a half." Later that night, I tuck them into bed and lay down to read a bedtime story. Elijah looks into my eyes and asks, "Are Dad's legs going to grow back?"

"No, honey, they don't grow back."

"Okay, I just don't want to talk about it anymore," as he rolls over and goes silent.

After an initial medical evaluation and surgeries in Germany, it's one a.m. when the casualty assistance officer calls and says, "I think you need to come." I don't need to hear more. I will be on the next flight to Germany, I assure them.

Monday morning, Nancy is at the EGL office early working on getting me and my mother on a flight to Germany, ASAP.

While Nancy deals with the airline, I drop the boys at daycare, explain the situation, and tell them I will call as soon as I have more information. Then I race to Walgreen's for a passport photograph before heading to the EGL office in Eagan.

Before I even reach the office, Jen has already collected more than $1,000 from co-workers. She deposits the money into my checking account then purchases several prepaid international phone cards. EGL CEO James R. Crane directs Human Resources to add a two-week bonus to my next paycheck.

At EGL, Lea Dale, one of our sales reps, grabs my arm and leads me to her car. Brad Schulke, a co-worker and friend since junior high school, comes along as they escort me to the Dakota County Service Center where my passport paperwork is processed in record time.

Almost without stopping to breathe, we drive to the Northwest Cargo terminal at Minneapolis/St. Paul International Airport and pass the documents off to another EGL staffer, Sue McGuire, who ensures that the documents are hand-carried by the next Northwest pilot departing for Chicago. The paperwork makes the one-hour trip to Chicago O'Hare Airport where a Chicago EGL staffer takes it from the pilot and races directly to the regional U.S. immigration office, literally walks it through the process, and streaks back to O'Hare in time to put it into the hand of the next pilot bound for Minneapolis. In less than a day, I have my passport and two tickets to Frankfurt, Germany. Nancy gets us on the nine-thirty p.m. Northwest Airlines flight to Frankfurt, via Amsterdam, first-class, for only the cost of tax.

Master Sergeant Brian Newcomer

I call Landstuhl and advise them of my travel itinerary, ask for an update on John, and then rush home to pack a suitcase for myself and also some clothes for the boys. They will be staying with Papa while my mom and I are in Germany.

At the airport, my mom and I are greeted by MSG Brian Newcomer, an Army casualty assistance officer (CAO) assigned to assist me. He comes aboard the same flight, but he gets stuck in the back of the plane.

Meanwhile, Nancy is just getting started. As soon as we depart for Germany, she launches a campaign asking EGL's 150 Minnesota employees to contribute cash and vacation days. With support from EGL CEO Jim Crane, her campaign literally goes global at EGL offices in every corner of the earth, touching ten thousand employees worldwide within minutes. What starts as an effort to garner two or three weeks of paid vacation turns into six months of vacation days donated by employees so that I can stay with John during his recovery.

Heading to Frankfurt on December 4, we consume most of a day in transit with the eight-hour flight to Amsterdam and another two-hour trip to Frankfurt, arriving early Tuesday. In Amsterdam, Mom and I are the first ones off the plane. Heading through the Jetway into the terminal, we find the doors locked. Initially, I figure the crew will come shortly, but Mom is becoming nervous and says, "We can't miss our flight to Germany."

"When is the flight?"

"We have less than an hour, and we need to go through customs."

I erupt in panic, screaming and crying for someone to open the Jetway doors into the terminal, jerking violently on the handles and repeatedly slamming my fist into the doors. Witnessing the crazy lady going postal before their eyes, wary passengers start backing away. I am about to go insane or get arrested when a very tall man with black wavy hair, dressed in a perfectly pressed, dark-blue dress suit, white shirt, and tie pushes through the crowd, gently taking my arm. "Mrs. Kriesel?"

"YES!"

The man introduces himself as the operations manager for Northwest Cargo and says, "Nancy Matthews with Eagle Global Logistics asked us to meet you and make certain that you get to your connection on time." He whisks us through customs and down to the plane with time to spare.

On arrival in Frankfurt, we are met by another Army casualty assistance aide who drives us to Landstuhl while Sergeant Newcomer rents a car and follows. Landstuhl Regional Medical Center is a permanent U.S. military facility located in Rhineland-

Pfalz, Germany, five miles south of Ramstein Air Base. It is the largest American hospital outside the United States, serving all service members and 44 coalition forces in Afghanistan, Iraq, Africa, Europe, and the Pacific, with a staff of 2,837 military and civilian medics, including 150 physicians, 250 nurses, and 40 Medical Service Corps officers. LRMC has 140 beds plus another 230 beds that serve outpatients from Iraq and Afghanistan.

I don't realize it at the time, but Newcomer has just become my personal angel, a tough, veteran soldier who would blush at the thought of being called my angel; but he is just that for the next few weeks, shattering barriers, ripping through red tape, and handling the seemingly trivial details that make life bearable.

We sit through a series of briefings that apparently are required but pretty useless inasmuch as I don't hear a word that is said. But it doesn't matter because I have Sergeant Newcomer to handle the details. The only thing I care about is seeing John, *right now!*

Newcomer begins paperwork for a special military insurance payout the Army provides to very seriously injured (VSI) soldiers. It's a bit tricky because John is the brigade's first VSI in this war; they have had a few KIA, but no VSI has survived. Together with the doctors, military insurance experts determine benefits based on anatomical loss of both feet.

Arriving at the intensive care unit, my heart stutters and I collapse in the doorway of John's room when I see that the damage he has suffered is far more shocking than anyone could have imagined. My mother and nurse Polly, who is hobbled by a cast for a broken ankle, catch me from behind. There is no way to prepare for how he looks; he's almost unrecognizable. His face is so swollen his eyes won't close. The doctors have coated his eyes with a gel to prevent them from drying out, but the pupils are rolled up out of sight and he looks dead. It's terrifying.

My mother is a nurse who tried her best to prepare me all the way across the Atlantic, "He's not going to look like what you expect." But it's still a shock. I take a second to catch my breath and then walk to his bed. I touch his hand gently and say his name. I tell him it's going to be okay now that I'm here, and I love him and I'm not going home without him.

I notice the small whiteboard stuck to the wall with John's name written in green dry erase marker across the top. Beneath it is every comment I had uttered on the phone to nurse Polly. She had taken it all down and relayed every comment to him. She even wrote, "Wife Katie, boys Brody and Elijah."

John is intubated and sedated with chest tubes, wires, and bandages, everywhere. His blood pressure is leaping up and falling down erratically; his face is swollen like a giant melon, and he is starting to become septic. Worse yet, he is not responding to the medications to control infection, and his right arm has developed a large, red welt that needs to be sliced open to reduce the potential for infection. Doctors fear he also has an infection from a perforated bladder suffered when he was eviscerated. He needs another surgery to remove debris from his wounds, but doctors are not sure that his body is ready for another surgery. They don't want to put him on the flight home until his blood pressure is stabilized.

In school I avoided science classes, but seeing John's arm slit open, exposing the muscles in his bicep, puts me right back in tenth grade health class. I know it shouldn't surprise me, but it does when I realize the inside of his arm looks just like those pictures in our textbook of pink muscle woven together like a sweater.

John is heavily sedated and not really conscious but does give off glimmers of hope to me by occasionally squeezing my hand, opening his eyes, and smiling a few times. Once he even mouths "I love you" through the tubes and bandages engulfing his face. He nods slowly in answer to the doctors' questions. It is just enough to let me know my guy is still in there. I sit there talking, but there is no response. "Okay, honey, if you are tired, just go to sleep. I'll just sit here."

A few seconds later, the nurse comes through asking, "John, are you awake." To my astonishment he nods, "yes." I guess I'll just be quiet for a while.

It turns out John was not alone while I raced around the world. We learn that LCpl. Bruce Miller, the Marine gunner in John's Humvee, was there with John; but Miller headed home to the United States just before we arrived. The nurse tells me Bruce talked constantly to John, and had her keep the television set on all the time tuned to sports because John is a sports nut. Without another word, she handed me two Minnesota National Guard shoulder patches and a note from Sergeants Rene Montero and Seth Steinbach, who wrote that they had been with John in Balad. One of John's surgeons, Dr. Bruce Bennett, who worked at St. Paul Regions Hospital in Minnesota before coming to Landstuhl, spotted the Minnesota Vikings tattoo on his right shoulder and started talking "Minnesotan" to him.

"Who else but a Minnesota guy would wear a Vikings tattoo?" Dr. Bennett asks me.

As we wait for surgery, I ask for a washcloth and clean his face. He still has dirt in his eyebrows and mud sprayed on his face from the explosion. At first I am angry to think that he is in his third emergency room and his face is still spotted with mud. But the medics and doctors were so focused on keeping him alive—the big picture— there wasn't time for presentation. I am here for the little things.

I think this is the third day; although, I have almost lost track. *Does time even matter?* I can't sleep or even think of being away from John. It's nearly four a.m., and the place is so quiet my soft-sole shoes are echoing in the hallways. I sit with John and start to wonder what is left of his legs. When a male nurse enters to check all the gauges, drips, and devices I inquire, "Can I see his legs?" He hesitates a second, cautions me that they are bandaged and not much to see. "Just hold my hand and let me see," I plead.

Even though I know what to expect, actually validating the loss is startling.

"I don't know anyone who is an amputee. Can they do anything with that one?" I point to his left stump, which is amputated a few inches above where his knee had been.

"I really don't know," he shows concern, "but if there is, they can do it at Walter Reed."

John's surgeon is adamant that he needs to get to Walter Reed as quickly as possible, but they keep pushing his surgery back, hoping each hour that John will be able to handle the added trauma to his body. Finally at ten p.m. they take him in. I sit in the waiting room, watching the clock creep ever so slowly minute after minute, hour after hour. The surgeon appears at three a.m.

"Surgery went fine and he has rebounded quite well. His blood pressure is stable; so, we're going to fly him to Walter Reed, right now."

Mom and I have open-ended return tickets, but I am scheduled to fly with John on the military transport until, at the very last minute, I am bumped to make room for another medical attendant. The commercial flight is now full, and I am going to be left behind in Germany for at least one more day. A quick call to Nancy in Minnesota, and in minutes I join Sergeant Newcomer and Mom on the Northwest flight to Amsterdam; sorry, but some standby passenger is back in the waiting area. Mother heads home to relieve Papa Harold in childcare duties while Newcomer and I wait for a flight to Dulles Airport in Washington, D.C. Northwest puts us in their VIP lounge until it's time to go.

Back home, Papa is busy trying to keep up with Elijah and Brody. He reports that all is going well unless you count getting Elijah's hockey pads on backward, but he is very eagerly anticipating Grandma Rita's return to Minnesota.

The blur continues to fog my mind as we touchdown in Washington, D.C., but Newcomer is there, grabbing a rental car and speeding us off to Walter Reed. We arrive at the hospital and are waiting when John's medevac ambulance, a big Bluebird school bus converted into an ambulance, arrives from Andrews Air Force Base with several wounded warriors.

Once John is checked into the hospital, the staff won't let me see him until they complete an initial assessment. I'm fine waiting, but Newcomer more or less forces me to leave for a few minutes. I have slept less than ten hours total in the past four days, including four or five on the plane and two in the hospital lounge. But I can't remember my last meal. Strangely, I am not hungry. Newcomer takes me to get settled in a room at the Walter Reed Guest House; however, I have no plans to sleep anywhere but in John's room.

Military accommodations often are not luxurious. I share a bathroom with somebody—don't know who is on the other side of the door to the adjoining room. I hope it's a woman, and I suspect the pink razor resting on the edge of the bathtub is a positive sign in spite of the stubble and dark ring lining the tub. Not so positive are the roach bait boxes and sticky pads for mice that are scattered about; hopefully not for rats. On the upside, I have a phone, computer, and a place to store things, even though I don't plan to sleep here.

As soon as my room is settled, Newcomer, himself a father of a four-year-old, starts playing dad and begins harping about my need to eat and get some rest... "if you're going to be of any help to John." He disappears for a few minutes and returns loaded down with one of every type of candy bar available in the vending machines. When I say I don't care for candy, he tosses them aside and drags me to the Subway restaurant embedded in the hospital. He "orders" me to eat at least half of a six-inch sub. Normally, I tend to be the one giving the orders and getting my way, but it's obvious this guy isn't going to yield. So I eat the sandwich and swallow a few sips of water.

It's approaching eleven p.m. when Newcomer urges me to get some rest and he heads off to the parking lot. I hate bugs of all shapes and sizes. I can't even stand ants; so, when I turn toward the bed and spot an enormous cockroach, the first cockroach I have ever seen, terror grabs me. The entire building gets a startling wake-up call as I streak down the hallway screaming at the top of my lungs for Newcomer. In semi-panic, I drag him back to where the creepy crawler has taken over the room.

"Wow, that is a big sucker," is all Newcomer says as he scoops up my luggage, grabs my arm, and leads me down to the Malogne

House where there is a front desk, just like checking into any big hotel. He calmly explains to the desk clerk what has happened in an attempt to get me a new room this late at night.

"What?" the guy behind the desk feigns surprise, and in my groggy, sleep-deprived state, he ignites my rage.

"Don't you dare act surprised," I blast away, cutting in front of Newcomer. "You've got bait boxes and sticky tape for mice and roaches all over that place; you know damn well they're there."

I check into Room 539 in Building 20, a much cleaner, larger space with a full-size bed instead of one twin, a clean bathroom, and, best of all, no bait boxes or sticky mouse traps.

John remains totally unconscious due to heavy sedation for the long flight home, and the Walter Reed Army Medical Center staff elects to keep him in the drug-induced coma. All I can do is hold his hand, lay my head against the railing at the side of his bed, and watch him breathe. His ICU room is a high-tech center with a mechanical bed and enough electronics, lights, machines, and equipment to rival the NASA command center, but nothing else. A nurse eventually slides a folding chair my way. The place is bright, busy, loud, chaotic, and always too hot or too cold, never comfortable.

Clocks are irrelevant in the ICU with treatments, surgeries, and tests going on all hours of the day and night. On John's first night at Walter Reed, I tag along with him for another CT scan and more x-rays. They move him into surgery to deal with skin that is growing around a drainage tube in his stomach, forming small pockets that are perfect hosts for bacteria and infection. Dr. Harold Frisch explains that they are still in the initial phase of assessing his injuries, and he anticipates some type of surgery will be performed on John at least every other day for the next week or two, depending on his condition and resilience. They plan to keep him on a respirator for the time being to reduce stress on his body during the surgeries.

"This is going to be a long process but, after the first six weeks, things should settle down greatly," Dr. Frisch counsels. Six weeks and things should settle down? That sounds like an eternity, but at least it sounds like hope.

"Mrs. Kriesel, John is going to remain sedated for a while. Why don't you go get settled into your quarters (that's military talk for room)." Back at the room, I pay our December bills—one less worry, but I have no plan to sleep anywhere but at the hospital.

Meanwhile, the busy Master Sergeant Newcomer is calling the Cottage Grove Police Department, asking them to check our house regularly. Apparently, some less-than-upstanding citizens have been burglarizing homes of injured soldiers, knowing that their families are away. Another prime target for these clever entrepreneurs is burglarizing homes during funerals for those who died in battle— *what kind of mind comes up with these demented schemes?*

Nancy emails that she has dug up details on the funerals for John's buddies Bryan McDonough and Corey Rystad and sent flowers as I requested with the message: "Our hearts are with you, SGT John Kriesel and Family."

Shortly after receiving Nancy's email, Master Sergeant Newcomer arrives and tells me that both families want to speak with me. I have no idea what to say. I can't even imagine what they are going through. As hard as this is, I still have John; but for John's sake I need to speak with them.

Sunday is another difficult day with a long surgery where the orthopedic surgeons clean and evaluate John's wounds, followed by ultrasound exams on his gallbladder and liver, and another CT scan of his wrist. When they are finished, he has tubes in his legs, right arm, and abdomen to permit drainage of excess fluid and blood, and to facilitate cleaning of the wounds. We get a better evaluation of his fractures, which include three separate breaks in his left arm, a shattered femur at the point of amputation in the left leg, and four separate breaks in his pelvis and lower back. That doesn't include several slices to the face and a severe cut down to the bone on his right wrist.

If there's any good news (at this point I am scrounging for every slice of good news they can find), some of the fear of internal damage has been lessened. The ultrasound discovered no stones or blockages that would inhibit his liver function or blood flow.

Master Sergeant Newcomer is back and takes me for a walk out in the Washington sunshine and fresh air. It's a refreshing moment. We discover a gym right across the street from my room where I can use my military ID for access to run off stress and anxiety while John is in surgery. I can't remember the last time I saw sunshine.

In the midst of chaos and sadness, there is hope for the future, and that prompts me to call Nancy for another favor—do a little Christmas shopping. John's memorial bracelet, wedding ring, and the cross he wore on his neck were cut off and lost in Iraq; so, I ask Nancy to replace his wedding band with a new one from Shane Co. and to add the inscription "My Husband—Hero—Hunna." Hunna is my special name for my honey.

Chapter 18

THE LONG ROAD TO
RECOVERY BEGINS

December 10, 2006

"John! Do you know where you are?" A voice drifts through the cloud that is beginning to clear asking me questions, but I don't recognize her voice.

"Germany?" I manage to exhale as my vision clears slightly and I see it is a nurse. Everybody goes to Landstuhl Regional Medical Center near Frankfurt, and I figure that is what happened to me.

"No John, you are in Washington, D.C., at Walter Reed Army Medical Center.

I'm pretty certain I know what happened; but I have been in a medically induced coma for eight days making it all feel like a dream, make that a nightmare. Reality jerks me conscious the instant I look down and confirm that my legs are gone, the left one above the knee, the right leg below the knee. This is no dream. I have so many questions.

"Where is Nelly?" I ask but she doesn't answer. I keep asking and telling her Nelson is my squad leader. Finally, she says she doesn't know about Nelson. Katie steps forward, and for an instant I wonder once again if this really is just a dream.

"Tim is still in Iraq, and he is going to be fine," she says.

"Do you know who this is?" the nurse interrupts.

"That's my wife." I nod, trying to smile.

"Can you tell me her name?"

Of course. What a stupid question. It's, ahhh damn, what is it? That's pretty bizarre. I can't remember her name. There's no way to fake it as I struggle for a name that I know as well as my own, while those big brown eyes plead with me to come up with the answer.

"KATIE!" I spit out, proud of having conquered the first of many, many challenges I am about to take on.

Memories of the blast surge back, stabbing me with the ferocity of another IED blast. "Did everybody make it out okay?"

Katie doesn't say a word, but the look on her face tells more than words. Tears of sadness escape from those eyes that had been smiling seconds before.

"I'm so sorry, honey, Corey and Bryan didn't make it."

A knife plunged into my chest couldn't inflict more pain. There are no words suitable to describe the sudden burst of emotion; it just sucks. Only moments ago, we were riding down Route Monterey, having a good patrol, joking and laughing. How can they be dead? I pretty much never cry, and suddenly I can't stop. I cry until my eyes are sore and red, but I can't wash away the sadness and pain, pain more intense than all of my physical wounds.

Most people have lost someone close to them—grandparent, aunt or uncle, friend ... not brothers ... at least not these kinds of brothers, brothers who know everything about you, the things you would never tell anybody else ... brothers who know your most embarrassing story, because they probably were there to see it first-hand. This is the worst kind of loss. Someone told me once, "Bad things happen to everybody. It is how you deal with the bad things that defines your true character." Every day I wonder why three of us survived, but Bryan and Corey didn't. It rips me apart, but it happened and I can't change it; it's time to show my true character. For their sake, I cannot waste my second chance at life.

Chapter 19

EUPHORIA GIVES WAY
TO REALITY

Euphoria at just being alive dissolves into dark reality when I realize I cannot move. I try to contemplate what lies ahead. All I ever wanted to be was a soldier, but I don't know any soldiers without legs.

I am conscious and alert, but obviously a bit confused after eight days in a coma, as a doctor appears. The short, slim doc pushes his glasses up as he bends over me and begins peppering me with questions about what happened. I stare up, focusing on an Ohio State pin proudly displayed on the collar of his white coat. The only thing I know about Ohio State is they always pound the Minnesota Gophers in football. But the doctor is no athlete; he's an Army second lieutenant doing his medical residency at Walter Reed.

"I need every little detail, John."

"I don't want to talk about it now."

"We need to know exactly how well you are recovering and the only way is for you to talk about it."

Even worse than the interrogation and memory testing is the ban on putting anything in my mouth, not even a sip of water. It's punishing, but I distract myself with television until the Army's newest commercial, "Army Strong," pops up and I ask Katie to find another channel. I don't know whether it's because I'm sad, scared, or just downright depressed; but I do know I just want to be back in Iraq, doing my job. The commercial is a painful reminder that Bryan and Corey are not coming back.

I had some long days in the desert when dust coated my throat, but suddenly drinking mud doesn't even seem as bad as the total ban on water at Walter Reed. They don't know how much damage has been done to my intestines and will not let me swallow anything before surgery. About the closest I come to a drink is when Katie is able to wet my lips with a damp sponge. God, I want to eat that sponge.

One of my first challenges, at least one of the first since regaining consciousness, is passing a test. And this is no multiple-choice job; it's an upper GI (gastrointestinal) or barium swallow to check out my interior plumbing. They wheel me into the barely illuminated, chalk-white room and slide me onto a table under a giant machine that looks like a CT scan. The worst part is just moving from my bed to the table. I feel the pain like a dozen sharp knives slashing into my shattered pelvis.

They dump two different flavors of barium down my throat. Neither will ever replace Gatorade. They stand fixed to the computer screen, watching the barium slide down my esophagus, run through my stomach, and ride into my intestines.

On a positive note, I am cleared to drink liquids. You cannot imagine how outstanding a glass of cool water can taste—no more feeding tube. Better yet, they bring me a glass of lemon-lime Gatorade with ice. I never knew anything could taste that good.

On December 11, a major milestone arrives as they roll me out of Ward 45A into Ward 45C, still in the intensive care unit, a very small step down or up—but progress. Ward 45A is one-to-one nursing care, while in 45C each nurse has three patients. The ward is one enormous room with a labyrinth of gray shower curtains carving out small cubicles for each patient. The only real downside is that my neighbor has a television set turned too loud to a program with car crashes and explosions, not something I want to hear. If I could move, I'd go rip the plug from the wall.

By the time I came out of the coma yesterday, the doctors had stabilized all of my wounds to stop the bleeding. My legs were starting to heal, although a constant battle with infection wages on. Gashes on my face were cleaned, and the damage to my intestines was temporarily repaired. Immediate attention focused on my mangled left arm and shattered pelvis.

So, today comes arm surgery. They wheel me into a gigantic surgical center. It's a virtual auditorium so large they could perform two or three surgeries at once with enough extra room for an orchestra. Well, maybe not an orchestra, but at least a radio is filling in background music as we enter. Pink Floyd is belting out "Time." Of all the millions of tunes in the world it strikes me as a very good sign that one of my favorite songs greets me in the operating room.

It's strange the perspective you get of a room while lying on your back. The room is mostly blue, a lot of blue offset by more stainless steel knives and tools than you will ever see at the Cutlery Store. Looking up, a curtain of long white gowns topped by a ring of eyes peering over green surgical masks; it's something from a horror film.

"John, we're going to move you from your bed onto the operating table," somebody interrupts my visual tour of the big room, "and it is going to hurt."

HURT! *Holy shit!* A bolt of lightning pierces my shattered pelvis and crushed arm as they lift me onto the table. I don't care how tough you are; this is almost more than I can handle.

Things don't improve much even when the medication begins to soften the bite of pain. My vision clears just enough to spot my x-rays hanging like a museum exhibit on a backlit wall display, somewhat fascinating, perhaps even artistic, if I didn't know what they are—pictures of my shattered arm from every angle imaginable; and no angle looks good. The arm is a jigsaw puzzle of broken pieces. I wonder how on earth they will be able to put it all together again. About that time everything fades from view and I am gone until much later.

When it's over they have my arm tied to an IV pole in an incredibly painful, uncomfortable position. With my busted pelvis, spine, and missing legs, I'm not going to be moving around a whole lot anyway.

Now that my left arm is reconstructed, using two eight-inch steel rods, pins, and staples, attention turns to the right arm, which is only slightly better. The bones aren't shattered but my right elbow is damaged. The bicep is torn and my wrist is slashed to the bone by the memorial bracelet I had been wearing in honor of SGT Matthew Commons, a soldier from Boulder City, Nevada, who died March 4, 2002, in Afghanistan.

I never knew Sergeant Commons, but we shared the bond of brotherhood in battle. Like most guys in Iraq, I bought the bracelet to honor a fallen soldier, grabbing his name at random. I remember checking details of his death on the Internet. Mostly, just looking at the bracelet in combat helped keep me focused on the reality of danger. I prayed no one I knew would ever have their name on a bracelet.

I'm making progress at Walter Reed. Today brought more success with a move from ICU into a private room in Ward 46, the Cardio Thoracic Surgery Ward where I have my own bathroom, not that I have any use for it. And, a real chair for Katie—a small recliner that tips back almost into a bed, quite the upgrade from a cold, metal, folding chair. Maybe she can finally get some sleep. Next we'll work on getting her to eat. Best of all, there is a phone in my room and I can call my boys every night at bedtime.

Doctors continue piecing me back together now that infection is somewhat under control, bleeding is stopped, and all of my injuries are stabilized. Tests reveal that my oxygen level is low, the result of a pulmonary embolism that was first discovered in the ICU. Every time I'm in surgery they try to deal with any infection and as many other issues as possible, multi-tasking at its best. This time they insert tiny "screens" in my vascular system to capture marauding blood clots that may break off from the embolism to explore my body, not something you want sneaking into your heart or brain.

Chapter 20

I Want to Talk to the Boss

Once I realize there truly is a life after near-death, albeit a tad different from the one I have known for my first twenty-five years, I decide it's time to talk with the boss. Every day, nurses pass through rattling off the same standard line, "Let us know if there is anything we can do for you." In my heavily medicated condition, I take them literally, not just: "How's your medication? Do you need another pillow or some water?"

"Absolutely! There is," I say, stopping one nurse dead in her tracks. She spins around and gives me a "did you say something" look.

"I need to see the boss."

"What?"

"I want to meet the president."

A startled, wide-eyed stare tells me, "Yah, right, whatever," without her even separating her lips. For more than a week, we replay the same crazy conversation, no matter who comes into my room.

"Let me know if there is anything you need."

"There is. I need to talk to the president."

Each day I become more insistent to the point they probably begin to think I want to scream at him. "Wait a minute," I plead.

"Here's the deal. I'm not mad at the president; I love the guy slightly less than I love my wife. I just want to meet him and say thanks for supporting us."

I barely finish my sentence when the phone rings—it's Governor Pawlenty. We have a good laugh, and he adds, "Sergeant, I just want to say how much the people of Minnesota appreciate your service, and to find out if there is anything we can do to help you."

"Yes, sir, there is one thing. When I get the Purple Heart, I want President Bush to pin it on me."

"John, I'll see what I can do about that."

Surgery is a regular routine throughout the month, rolling down to the blue room every other day to clean out infection in one place or another. Anyone who has ever had surgery for skin cancer has a general idea what it's like. They keep cutting away infected skin and tissue and testing it until there is no sign of infection. It's a slow process because they don't want to take any more than necessary, but they need to get every last trace of infection. It seems to take forever.

Doctors make major progress December 15 when they complete repair on both legs and zip up the wound in my abdomen, but the damage and constant trauma resulting from repairs tends to encourage development of blood clots. Hopefully, the filters in my blood stream snare the clots before they cause any damage.

Then a setback occurs. The 48-hour bacterial cultures taken after leg surgery come back positive for the left leg.

Chapter 21

DOCTOR THINKS
I MAY NOT WALK

After resting up over the weekend, Monday, December 18, is a huge day. My pelvis and lower spine were shattered in the blast, and the doctors decide the only option is to fuse them together. One little problem, while spinal fusion surgery is not uncommon, surgery of this magnitude has only been tried twice anywhere in the world. Even if successful, they warn, I most likely will spend the majority of my time in a wheelchair because spinal fusion will cause up to fifty percent loss of mobility in the lower back preventing a normal walking gait. Even walking with prosthetics will be very difficult, but with a lot of physical therapy and help from God, walking remains on the possible list. That's all I need—is a tiny shot at hope.

Going in, they tell Katie the back surgery probably will be nine hours, but this is new territory even for a medical team that has pretty much seen it all. As with everything there is good news and bad news.

Luckily, I am unconscious in the operating room when things go from bad to worse. My back injuries are even more severe than anticipated, requiring a dozen stainless steel screws with the possibility of more surgery and more screws in the future to hold the breaks in place. If there is anything good about the surgery, it is that the back specialist, who is on hand to deal with any leaks in spinal fluid, is not needed. Despite the extent of damage, surgeons say they are pleased with the result. Surgeons always say they're pleased, no matter what happens.

After a while I begin to feel like a classic car with mechanics crawling around my chassis, tweaking this, tightening that, and cleaning up any leaks. While they have me on the lift, overhauling my drive shaft, they clean up the lingering source of infection in my left leg. The leg is getting much better. The swelling is down significantly.

Back surgery requires that I spend the next twelve weeks lying flat on my back, very limited movement, no weight bearing. Worse still, for the next few days I cannot eat or drink anything; all sustenance will be from intravenous fluids. Overriding everything, doctors say the surgery was a success, naturally. With the back surgery completed, I move to Ward 68, a general surgery ward.

That's the good news. The bad news: Katie begins to focus on the doctor's pre-surgery explanation that "Walking most likely won't be John's primary mode of movement and he is going to require at least eighteen months in recovery and rehabilitation."

She's a very strong person, but that statement crushes every ounce of strength lingering in her overly exhausted brain, igniting a rainforest of tears that persists through the night, calming only slightly to partly cloudy by the time I awake.

"What's wrong?" I inquire.

Reluctantly she reveals the grim medical prognostication.

"Are you kidding?" I muster all the strength I can manage, putting on the best face possible, "I'm going to walk and I'm not going to be in this damn hospital for eighteen months."

I don't know if I actually believe the drivel spilling out of my mouth, but Katie is eager to grab anything good. My bold declaration trips her giggle button. She morphs from morose to giddy and is practically bouncing with joy when she talks by phone to her good friend and boss Nancy Matthews. Nancy is busy collecting daily updates from Katie, Katie's mother Rita, and whoever has the latest news that she can spread by email throughout the EGL family.

"Yesterday, when Katie shared news about John's surgery, she was devastated," Nancy wrote to the Eagle Global Logistics staff in her December 19 email. "This morning, after talking to John, she is giggling and upbeat. He is her true inspiration. John is high on life and remains feeling very blessed that he is alive and has his family."

"Aunt" Nancy is like a big sister or ad hoc mother helping with anything that comes up in addition to keeping everyone up-to-date on the latest Kriesel news. Early Wednesday (December 20) she arrives at Grandpa Harold and Grandma Rita's house to find Elijah and Brody standing in the driveway armed with suitcases and backpacks ready to move out.

"Aunt Nancy, are we going in a big, big, big airplane?" Elijah blurts with uncontrolled excitement.

"Aunt Nancy, is my dad at the airport?" Brody jumps in before Elijah finishes.

"Is my mom there? How long will it take?"

Grandma Rita stumbles out the door still half-asleep and reveals to Aunt Nancy that she was awakened at four a.m. to find Elijah and Brody standing next to her bed, holding up their calendar.

"Is this the day?"

"Yes, this is the day."

Elijah doesn't like heights so the thought of flying up in the sky is making him nervous. But his excitement for the trip outweighs his fear. A couple of cuddly teddy bears, provided by an EGL staffer as flight buddies, help distract him further. Elijah names his bear "Jet" and Brody dubs his "Cody."

Like the boys, I'm awake at four a.m. with a little help from the doctors making their early morning rounds. I'm just as excited about their arrival as they are to make the trip.

Once again the good news, bad news bears rise up when doctors spot infection on my right leg. Quickly unscheduled surgery is booked for later in the day to clean up both legs, an almost-routine occurrence at this point. The good news: no spike in my temperature.

When I awake from surgery, my constant companion Katie is there with news that Brody and Elijah are on their way. Their arrival throws Katie into a storm of anxiety as she faces the need to prepare them for what they are about to see. She has talked with a child psychologist several times preparing for their visit. But this isn't rehearsal; this is facing her toughest audience.

"Tell them what a hospital room looks like, the things they will see. Tell them what John has on him, bandages, casts, stitches, tubes, and the machines. Just describe what it looks like so they don't walk in there and get surprised," the doctor stresses to Katie in each meeting.

Before the boys come, Katie realizes her room in Building 20 with one bed isn't large enough. When she wanted a bigger room in Malogne House after the cockroach incident she was told those rooms are for families. So, she heads back to the front desk where she explains that the boys are coming and she needs a larger room.

When Katie's parents arrive with Brody and Elijah, she brings the boys to the hospital lobby and launches into the lecture she has been rehearsing in her head for days. "Boys, before we go up to see your dad I have some big stuff to tell you. Dad has a lot of bandages on his arms and legs and his tummy, and he has a really cool bed with lots of buttons."

Katie gets creative: "Spiderman was a regular man when he was bitten by a spider and he got super powers. Daredevil got blinded and then he got super powers. Dad is getting new legs, so he will be Super Dad."

I never do find out if they bought that; hopefully, they don't expect me to start leaping tall buildings in a single bound or running faster than a speeding bullet—but, hey, maybe with some adjustments to my bionic legs, who knows?

"Okay, okay, Mom," Brody interrupts. "We just want to go see Dad."

That was that.

Maybe I am more nervous than anyone, make that terrified, of what the boys are going to think. They peek cautiously into my room. Almost by instinct I pull a blanket over the stumps that had once been legs.

"You don't need to cover your ovals, Dad," Elijah's little voice slashes through the tension, "I'm just glad you're alive."

Those words lift me to the top of the mountain. It's amazing how a child can strip away all the crap in life and slice right to the heart of any issue. Elijah opens my eyes and my heart, in an instant telling me that I am going to be okay. This little guy just taught me that no matter how I look or how badly I am injured my boys still love me and look at me as the same old dad—the definition of unconditional love.

Elijah moves quickly to my side, but Brody hesitates in the doorway, scanning the shape in the bed, all the medical machines, wires, gauges, lights, and beepers that fill this strange place. Despite his mother's attempts to describe what was ahead he appears startled by the sight.

"Hey, guys, come on in," I try to put a smile in my voice.

That's all it takes. Brody hears the same old voice, and he knows in an instant that everything is okay. At that moment I truly start to believe that I am going to be okay; I have to make it for these guys and for Katie.

"Dad, you've got some really nice ovals," Elijah declares as he closely explores what remains of my legs and the perfect "ovals" formed by the bandages. Inspecting me from end to end, he pauses for close examination of my right arm where the bicep had been split open and stitched back together. A giant smile erupts, "Good, Dad, they didn't sew over your Vikings tattoo."

Once more, in preparation for another round of surgery, I can't drink anything. Katie hands each of the boys a cup with Gatorade and some sponge swabs so they can take turns giving me a "drink." They carefully dab the delicious syrup on my lips, and their faces light up with joy; it's very cool. The guys also manage to dribble Gatorade all over my face, down my neck, and around the bed— every errant drop draws a chorus of giggles until it's obvious they are performing for their small audience. They are just being little boys, and that is great medicine.

"Hey, what's that?" Elijah points to the bag of yellow liquid.

Katie and I exchange furtive glances and then, while I contain myself to a mild smile, she explains, "The doctors gave Dad a hose to pee in so that he doesn't have to get out of bed every time he has to go."

"Wow! That's cool," the boys say in unison.

A nurse interrupts our urine discovery talk to show us a photograph of President George Bush running on the White House lawn with a wounded soldier who has prosthetic legs.

"Cool," they proclaim. With all the new discoveries at the hospital, most of what they are learning is indeed pretty cool.

After staring at the photograph for quite some time, Brody calmly announces that he wants "those cool legs, just like Dad."

I explain that only people who lost their legs get those new special legs, but they are indeed pretty cool because they never wear out. Brody runs a hand down his right leg and announces, "I need a new one because this one doesn't work so good."

His impish smile betrays his humor before I can react.

"Where's your wheeler chair?" Elijah changes direction. "We want to ride in the wheeler chair with you." Unfortunately, back surgery keeps me in bed; the wheeler chair ride will need to wait for another day.

The next morning Grandpa Harold visits with me while Katie and her mother take the boys to see a bit of Washington, D.C. Along the way they stop at the military barber shop in the hospital for haircuts "just like Dad's."

One of the nurses commandeers a recliner that folds out into a small bed and works well for two little boys who spend long periods each day for a week telling me stories, watching cartoons on television, and listening while I read to them. At one point Brody asks if he can get into bed with me. My nurse reflects instant concern, but I figure what can a four-year-old do that a two hundred-pound bomb hasn't done already. He climbs in and his warm little body is the perfect tranquilizer. Elijah wants to climb into bed as well, but he hesitates with concern that it might hurt me. Concern evaporates into a giant smile as I look his way and give him the okay to crawl in next to me.

A couple positive steps occur in the good news, bad news march. They haul me down to x-ray and discover that my pelvis is healing well enough for me to sit up just a bit, about twenty degrees. More good news: exploratory surgery reveals no more infection in the left leg, and the right is cleaned up with antibiotic beads inserted. The beads cut infection much like a timed-release weed killer. They say my legs are healing better than expected and the tissue looks healthy.

Cut it just like Dad's

Little boy therapy

Chapter 22

THE PRESIDENT VISITS

It turns out Katie and Rita know about the president coming a day early but they don't tell me for fear that something will change and they know I would be seriously disappointed. I may be busted up and under heavy meds, but my brain is not completely gone. When Rita and Harold arrive with the boys at seven-thirty a.m., I figure something is up. The nursing staff confirms that the president is coming, and they push me and my bed to another room that is completely stripped of all equipment, making room for the presidential entourage and my family.

We're barely settled into the new room when I notice guys in dark suits roaming the hallway, several of them leaning into the room and scanning the area just as we had been taught to survey a suspicious building before entering. It gets me thinking it must be soon. (Secret Service locked down the floor three hours before the president was due to arrive.) Finally, a guy who lacks the intensity of the dark suits ambles in, smiles, and surveys the scene. The big Nikon camera dangling around his neck is the clincher. "He's coming soon."

I look at Katie as though I have just won the Indianapolis 500. "Did you hear that? He's coming. I guess Governor Pawlenty did the job."

We discover that "soon" apparently means different things to different people as the hours drag on and we don't dare venture out of the room for fear "He" will arrive at that moment.

The wait is long and painful. At times I fear he has changed his mind or something big happened that called him away, or maybe he just doesn't have enough time for everyone. Just when despair is beginning to creep into my head, a couple of guys who are either Jehovah Witness volunteers or Secret Service agents poke their heads into the open doorway, sweep the room with radar scan vision, and vanish. Two other agents step in. Ten seconds later "he" bolts through the doorway with that rapid pace you see on television when he strides across the White House lawn to his helicopter, and he shoots right up to my bedside.

"How are you doing, Sergeant?"

"I'm great, sir. Sir, I want to thank you for all that you do to support all the troops over there. Your leadership means a lot to us."

"It's your country that thanks you, Sergeant."

"Attention to orders!" commands one of the guys standing behind the president. I can't quite snap to attention, but I give it my best effort as he reads the citation:

To all who shall see these presents, greetings.

This is to certify that the president of the United States of America has issued the Purple Heart to Sergeant John M. Kriesel for wounds received in action near Fallujah, Iraq, on December 2, 2006. Given under my hand in the city of Washington, this 22nd day of December 2006, signed Francis J. Harvey, Secretary of the Army.

The president of the United States leans over my bed and pins the Purple Heart on my chest.

I still can't sit up because of my crushed pelvis and spinal injuries. He smiles broadly, shakes my hand, and gives Katie a hug. The president turns to Brody and Elijah, drops down on one knee, puts his arms around them like any grandfather, and looks directly into their eyes. "Are you proud of your dad?"

"Yes," they respond in unison.

"Good. You should be. He is a hero."

I am no hero. I was just in the wrong place at the wrong time but, wow, watching the president of the United States say that to my sons and my wife will sustain and motivate me forever.

Wrapping an arm around Katie, the president gives her a warm hug and whispers, "Hang in there."

Katie's mother, Rita, shares grandmother thoughts with Laura Bush as Katie and I talk to the president. We can feel Laura's pain and compassion. Later we talk about how difficult it must be for them to visit so many severely wounded soldiers. It's a tremendous boost to our spirit to have them take the time and show true compassion.

Then as suddenly as Santa Claus vanishes up the chimney, the president is gone leaving me in a daze. Brody breaks the spell with his little four-year-old voice, "So, is George Washington leaving?"

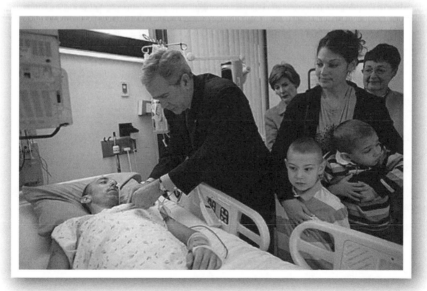

President Bush pins the Purple Heart on my chest

Chapter 23

CHRISTMAS 2006

Strange as it may sound, this is the best Christmas of my life.

The boys and Katie's parents arrive loaded with enough holiday decorations to outfit most of the hospital. They are having a grand time hanging it all in my room along with decorating a little Christmas tree that Nancy Matthews sent. The centerpiece is a giant snowflake with a photograph of the boys.

I'm dumbfounded when a truckload of gifts from the Chicago office of Eagle Global Logistics appears. Here's a bunch of people who work for the same company as Katie. They don't actually know us, but look at what they have done. They collected enough money to buy all these gifts, wrapped them with care, and shipped them to EGL's Baltimore office where a driver brought them to Walter Reed. How do you say "thank you" for that? Maybe the electricity generated by the boys can be felt all the way to Chicago; it certainly pumps up my spirit to an all-time high.

Santa's bag unveils Game Boys, portable DVD players (the boys quickly dub them "little TVs"), Batman and Superman laptops, and Transformers (the movie-inspired model cars that morph into super heroes). I'm almost as excited as the boys because the earlier 1980s version of Transformers was my favorite toy. Before they unwrap each box, they carefully position it next to an ear and shake, then announce with unbridled joy, "It doesn't feel like clothes!"

The gifts are all so spectacular it's difficult to focus on one, but the boys are particularly impressed with their new "Megazoid." Elijah exclaims that the new "Operation Overdrive" cartoon won't be on television until February; so, he is quite certain that he and Brody are the "very first ones" to get that special toy. I'm just trying to figure out what language they are speaking.

Katie and I unwrap a Trivial Pursuit 1980s game, and she confesses that she put it on her wish list. "While you're drugged up I may actually have a chance at winning."

Keeping with the game mode I receive a handheld electronic Jeopardy game. Katie thought that would be perfect therapy to strengthen my arms and improve manual dexterity in my hands.

We got married at Christmas time; so, for the holidays, we also get to celebrate our anniversary. Katie hands me a tiny box, and I confirm the old adage that the best things come in small packages as I pull out a beautiful wedding ring to replace the one that had been cut from my finger at the Al-Taqqaddum Hospital in Iraq.

Just to prove that great minds, or is it great lovers, think alike; I reach under my pillow and produce a similar sized box for Katie that also contains a ring set with a series of small, gleaming diamonds for her right hand. Pulling that off was a major tactical procedure accomplished with the assistance of "Aunt" Nancy. I had been talking on the phone with Nancy one day when Katie stepped out of the room for a few seconds, giving me just enough time to place the order. As it turns out, Nancy was secret shopper for both Katie and me.

The boys echo my thoughts about Christmas, although for slightly different reasons. "Dad, this is the best Christmas ever. We got everything on our list, everything and more! And, we didn't get any clothes. Yeah!"

"I guess we better not give them clothing for Christmas anymore," Katie whispers in my ear with a patented Katie giggle. In the past, Christmas was usually a good time to replenish outgrown duds for two highly active, rapidly growing guys. We definitely need to work on a new holiday giving plan.

Christmas day turns into a military parade with one dignitary after another roaming the halls, talking to the troops. Among the many people stopping by my room that day are more stars than the Milky Way. These constellations all sit atop the shoulders of high-ranking military officers. Each general has a pocket full of custom, embossed coins to hand out to the troops, and I acquire a whole collection.

President Bush's chief of staff, Joshua Bolten, stops in and gives Katie a business card with his personal contact information, asking her to call him as soon as I am ready to visit the White House. He promises a personal tour of the White House, including the West Wing.

Mixed in with all the stars, bars, and brass buttons, my chief orthopedic surgeon, Dr. Kyle Potter, slips into the room, bearing a gift himself: a T-shirt emblazoned with the words "Life is Good."

"I thought of you the second I saw this," Dr. Potter says.

Nothing is ever perfect in this crazy world, and even this perfect day suffers a blemish when a news reporter manages to call my room, doing a "Christmas wrap-up on Minnesotans in the War." After agreeing not to ask about Bryan or Corey, she jumps right into asking how I feel today about losing two close friends. I start to respond and break down in tears. Pulling myself together, we redo the interview after she promises me that she will not use the part where I choked up. Of course, when it hits the air, my crying *is* the focus of the story.

Chapter 24

RECOVERY BEGINS TO TAKE HOLD

For now, it's back to business, and that means more surgery. One day after Christmas and I am heading into the operating room for my 3,000-mile grease and oil change; actually, just a bacteria and infection inspection on my legs. Surgeons find a bit of infection has wormed its way into my right leg, but overall they say they are pleased that the muscle, bone, and tissue are all healthy. Another milestone along the tedious trail to recovery comes when they remove all the stitches in my upper body.

Soldiers are supposed to be brave, and I am trying, but there are times that truly test a man's spirit, especially the frequent trips to surgery. Surgeries are working well, and I am improving every day, but I am starting to hate being put to sleep in that massive, sterile blue room under those scorching, bright lights with a crowd of white-clad beings peering down at me.

It may be irrational, but every time I start to go under, I fear I may not wake up. Katie asks the doctors if it would be helpful to increase my medication before surgery so that I can avoid even seeing the operating room. They concur. They also allow her to be with me in the surgical prep room until I drift off into dreamland before rolling into the operating room.

"John, you have some bone growth on your legs," Dr. Kyle Potter enters Room 5735 displaying a strange, translucent plastic object resembling a piece of pink coral. Wow! Maybe Elijah had it right about growing new legs.

Unfortunately, the growth is neither sufficient nor structurally sound, but apparently it is a strange medical development occurring among American and British soldiers who suffer traumatic physical damage in Iraq. For some yet-to-be-learned reason, the incidence of sudden bone growth following severe bone injury is much higher among soldiers, roughly sixty-four percent, than in the civilian population. So unusual is this phenomenon that medical experts throughout the world are studying it, attempting to learn why it is happening. Officially dubbed "heterotopic ossification," HO for us ground pounders, the condition was written up in *The Journal of Bone and Joint Surgery* by a team of doctors, including my guy, CPT Benjamin Kyle Potter, MD.

Dr. Potter's strange plastic model is something special, a very expensive one-of-a-kind chunk of plastic replica of my leg and another of my spine and pelvis. Walter Reed is one of the few places in the world using the new technology to create precise 3-D bone models before making a single surgical cut. The system, originally designed for the manufacturing industry, takes a massive series of CT scans that are analyzed and cleaned up by computer and then fed into a machine called the SLA 7000. The machine holds a 320 kilogram vat of liquid resin with a laser system that slices across the vat one-tenth of a millimeter at a time, bonding resin into the exact shape desired. The process can take up to fifty hours and is followed by a not-so-scientific clean-up process. That final phase requires an experienced prosthetics technician using dental picks to clean out the cracks and crevices.

The resulting precise model of my leg is valuable because it shows

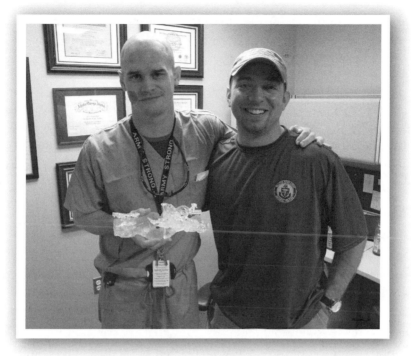

Dr. B. Kyle Potter displays a precision 3-D bone model

Dr. Potter exactly how to remove the extraneous bone growth before he makes the first cut, and that will reduce damage and minimize time that the wound has to be open, thereby reducing the risk of infection. Even better, examination of the model convinces him that surgery is not necessary.

"We'll just monitor the extraneous bone growth and tough it out," explains my prosthetist, Tom. What he means is he will do the monitoring while I do the toughing out. He says wearing the prosthesis and walking eventually will wear out the nerve endings and I will get used to it. The HO is extremely painful. At first it irritates the tissue so badly that merely touching the area sends fire up my leg.

Several weeks of bed restrictions lie ahead, but patience is not one of my strong suits. I decide to use this time to get a jump on de-sensitizing my stumps. For the next few weeks, I ask Katie to smear lotion on the areas over the bone growth, press down as hard as she can until I can't take anymore, and rub the scars on my legs vigorously so that they get used to pressure. There isn't a dictionary available with words sufficient to describe the pain; but it needs to be done, and it's working.

Throughout the process, Dr. Potter and his partner, Dr. Timothy Mickel, a Navy Lieutenant Commander, are my primary surgeons, although there is a constant parade of doctors, nurses, and technicians. Mickel is a jokester, constantly doing something goofy or talking sports, both of which lift my spirits. I swear he just walked off the set of *Scrubs*.

"He is the man," Dr. Mickel declares one morning as Dr. Potter leaves the room. "You need to understand that what Potter explains to you, every doctor knows in medical terms, but he can explain it to anyone. The guy is really, really smart."

Their boss, Dr. Frisch already had told us the same thing. But Dr. Potter is so humble and easygoing that we can talk to him like a friend. Even the most obscure terms and procedures are understandable when described by Dr. Potter.

Every day a pack of doctors and interns roams the halls, doing their rounds, sweeping into my room, where they carry on a discussion in some foreign language as they poke, prod, and check out every inch of my body. While Dr. Potter updates everyone on my condition and any surgical plans, the others mumble words I've never heard and can't pronounce. They nod their heads in unison like a rack of bobblehead dolls and vigorously scratch notes in their little blue books; then the herd shuffles off to the next room.

Chapter 25

NELLY COMES TO THE RESCUE

"Hey, Kries. It's Nelly," the phone voice announces as clearly as if he is standing next to me. In Iraq, SSG Tim Nelson was my roommate and squad leader, the guy who was doing anything he could just to keep me alive the last time I heard his crazy voice while they loaded my broken body into the helicopter twenty-two days ago—*God, is that all?* It seems like I have spent a lifetime in this bed, but it has only been twenty-two days, eight of which I don't remember at all. It must have been longer.

"Kriesel, I hear that Katie has been doing nothing but looking out for your lazy ass 24/7. It's time she gets out of there for something special."

Nelly lived in Washington, D.C., for a few years when he was in the active Army with the "Old Guard" serving as the escorts to the president. He provided security and honor guards for presidential events and state dinners at the White House, ceremonies at the Tomb of the Unknown Soldier, and visits of foreign dignitaries at the Pentagon. Among his more interesting duties was entertaining the president's dogs by tossing a tennis ball back and forth at events on the White House lawn during state visits.

"I made arrangements at the best salon in Washington, D.C., for Katie to have their finest four-hour spa treatment complete with massage, facial, manicure, pedicure, haircut, and styling for your anniversary. She'll probably resist, but you need to make sure that she goes. Tell her it's paid for and there are no refunds."

How's that for a great friend? Nelly was right. Katie doesn't want to go, doesn't think she needs it, and is uncomfortable leaving me alone. My dad solves the alone part immediately by agreeing to keep me company. She waivers a bit until I insist.

"It was wonderful," Katie smiles and gives me a hug when she returns. Somehow she doesn't seem to be in the wonderful mood I expected, and, after repeated questioning, she admits the best part was knowing that Tim really cared. The day itself was a total disaster that put her into tears more than once. She had not left the hospital for a minute since arrival, other than brief trips to her room or to eat, and she felt guilty about "wigging out" by being gone so long.

Just getting to the spa was a monumental task that started with an argument with the duty officer at Soldier Family Assistance Center (SFAC) in an attempt to get a taxi voucher, and culminated standing outside on K Street in downtown Washington, D.C., without a coat, in freezing weather, waiting for the taxi that took forty minutes to respond.

"The people at the salon were so funny," Katie says. "You can come back some other time they told me when I said I had to leave before I was finished."

Maybe someday a few years from now we'll stop in and take them up on the offer.

For now we relax and take comfort in what Tim was able to accomplish by long distance. That's just the kind of guy Tim Nelson is, a big-hearted guy caught in the middle of the Iraq tragedy, just as he was an eyewitness to the disaster of September 11, 2001, while participating in riot training at Fort Myer in Washington, D.C. Fort Myer adjoins Arlington Cemetery, sitting on a hill overlooking the Pentagon. At the time, 3rd Infantry was preparing for mammoth crowds of protestors from throughout the world that were expected to haunt the International Monetary Fund and World Bank Annual Meeting September 28 to October 4.

Nelly didn't see the Boeing 757, American Airlines Flight 77, slam into the Pentagon, but he heard it and watched in horror from less than a mile away as smoke and flames erupted, killing all sixty-four people on the plane (six crew, fifty-four innocent passengers, and four highjackers) and 126 in the Pentagon. The plane had departed Washington Dulles Airport heading to Los Angeles with ten thousand gallons of jet fuel shortly before slamming into the west side of the Pentagon at 345 mph, puncturing through rings E, D, and C. Intense fire held rescue teams and firefighters at bay for several hours. As horrific as the terrorist attack on the Pentagon was, it would have been far worse were it not for the fact that the two areas adjacent to the crash site were closed in preparation for renovation.

Within minutes Nelson and the 3rd Infantry were dispatched to the Pentagon for search, rescue, and security duty. "Once we were able to enter, we looked for survivors, but in the area of the crash no one was left alive," Nelson said. He described how bulletproof windows designed to protect workers inside the Pentagon were scarred and scratched on the inside by panicked victims attempting without success to break out by repeatedly slamming chairs against the windows.

"I saw one incredibly weird sight right in the center of the building where the plane punched through the outside ring," he recalled. "In the midst of total devastation, there was a guy sitting in a chair seemingly untouched except that he was dead. He looked like a department store mannequin on display. Nearby a woman was lying under a desk as though she had just fallen asleep. Not a scratch on either of them right in the center of massive devastation. Everything around them was burned, melted, twisted, and destroyed."

The next day Nelson was searching for victims when President George W. Bush arrived to survey the catastrophe and to meet rescuers who stood at attention while the president shook every hand and thanked each soldier.

"Mr. President," one guy spoke up. "Sir, what are we going to do? What do you think?"

"This really pisses me off," the president said with conviction. "We're going to get the people who did this."

Soldiers spent two days searching for victims and then turned to the grim task of removing bodies and fragments of the plane. Nelson said plane parts were taken to tents set up on the grounds by the FBI to reconstruct the aircraft. For the recovery operation, Nelson and the others donned full-body, white DuPont recovery suits with booties and facemasks. Suited up, the soldiers looked like a pack of giant rabbits moving through the colorless charred debris.

Whether searching for survivors in the Pentagon, looking after his Joes in battle, or doing good deeds for wounded warriors, Nelly is always looking out for others, especially Katie and me. He's more than a leader; he is the definition of a friend.

Chapter 26

NO NEED FOR FLIP FLOPS

December 29, 2006

In recovery, progress is defined by minor events. Just exercising my arms to begin rebuilding strength in my upper body is that kind of event, made especially challenging by the fact that I cannot move my medically repaired back, although I am able to sit up at a twenty-degree angle. That may not sound like a big deal, but try lying flat on your back for nearly two weeks. It's a big deal. Dr. Kyle Potter says that's the way it will be for the next twelve weeks while my fused spine and pelvis heal.

That's today's somewhat good news. Aside from the lack of any mobility and the need to avoid movement in my lower body, there is the bladder issue—perhaps that's more than you want to know. Suffice it to say that Katie must be getting close to a nursing degree by now. While most people would disappear at the mere thought of a colostomy bag, my girl not only stayed but she learned how to change the bag for me. That is what you call true love.

Lying in a hospital bed at Walter Reed isn't as boring as you might think. Katie is always there keeping me happy and entertained, and there is a steady stream of visitors—many of them famous celebrities, others are just good people giving their time. Mixed in with all the famous folks, the charge nurse, Scuba Steve, stops by with a gift certificate for Subway and a box of Godiva chocolates. Somebody told him it was our anniversary today. Normally I might not rate Subway at the top of my dining choices, but it is the only non-chowhall option in the building and that makes it our special place.

A little lady with a big heart slips into the room, careful not to disturb anyone. Hesitant at first, she quietly inches forward and hands Katie a gift bag from the American Red Cross. She has the quiet demeanor and characteristics of a small-town school teacher with her roller-style hair and reading glasses that dangle from a gold chain.

"Oh, John," Katie begins pulling things from the gift bag. "A T-shirt and boxer shorts. Hope they fit. Hey, here's some candy and, oh my gosh, a pair of flip flops. These will make great shower shoes when you get to take your own shower." Even as the word shower tumbles across her lips our eyes meet and she freezes for just a second before we both break into laughter.

"I'm thinking I probably won't be needing those," I manage between laughs.

We keep the flip flops just for fun.

Chapter 27

HAPPY NEW YEAR 2007

My new motto is: "Life is good," just like it says on the T-shirt Dr. Potter gave me for Christmas. And, the New Year definitely arrives with plenty of good cheer. Dr. Mickel and Dr. Potter, always the bearers of good news and bad news, say the infection is contained in both legs and healing is proceeding better than they expected. Dr. Potter slides a "shrinker sock" on my right leg to reduce swelling and begin the process toward the day when I can be fitted for prosthetic legs.

More good news: staples closing the incision in my back are removed and the abdominal wounds are healing "very well."

It's weird, but occasionally I get what they call "phantom pain" in my missing legs. I hate that term, phantom pain; so, I just describe the sensation. It feels as though someone is cutting my foot off. The feeling is very real but is obviously not accurate. On second thought, perhaps phantom pain doesn't sound so bad.

Lying on my back twenty-four hours a day has generated a pressure sore on my lower back, right on my tailbone. That is a new area of concern. Fortunately, my back has healed enough that I can be turned ever so carefully on my side, but only on the right side. If I try to lie on the left side with my short leg, the lack of support twists my back and causes even more pain.

It's been more than a month since the blast although I could swear it has been a year. There must be some positives. Let's see, it's not 130 degrees, I wake up looking at my wife, I talk to my kids every day, and there is no fear of bullets or bombs. But I worry every day for my brothers still in Iraq. My new reality is the fear of just going to sleep. I just can't shake that irrational fear that I might never wake up again, but Katie is the ultimate medicine. I tell her to leave all the lights on and keep the TV on. I can't stand quiet or dark.

As for medicine, recovery spawns new levels of pain, something I could never have imagined. Dilaudid is no longer sufficient to ease the bite; so, Dr. Janze prescribes methadone, and the first night I sleep eleven hours. I haven't slept more than a few hours at a time in more than a month; perhaps being in a coma for eight days, I stored up some sleep credits.

Nothing can ever be perfect. While the methadone eases my pain, it stirs up an intense bout of nausea that in turn requires still another drug. Who needs food when you get forty pounds of pills a day? Speaking of pills, they adjust the level of medication for the pain in my missing legs and that seems to be working.

A volunteer with Soldiers' Angels, a nonprofit group working in the hospital, comes by after talking with Nancy Matthews and tells us how their mission is to help soldiers by providing computers, computer repair, voice-activated computers, and other personal services. They want to donate one of their computers to us. Instantly, we have access to the outside world and discover that it is still out there.

For more than a month, my world has been encased in a ten-by-twenty-foot space with little more than tubes, wires, blinking lights, and chirping machines stuffed between four cream-colored walls. A window and a door offer hints that the world is still out there, but the fleeting view as people flash by is a little like watching it on television. The computer unleashes actual contact and interaction with real human beings, people I know.

When you can't get off your back, it helps just to know that people remember your name. Today that's not a problem. The phone is ringing off the wall, and my computer is lit up with emails talking about front page stories in the Minneapolis *Star Tribune* and St. Paul *Pioneer Press* as well as *MSN News* online and a blog I am writing for KARE-TV, an NBC affiliate in Minneapolis-St. Paul.

"John, have you thought about what we can do with the house?" Katie jerks me back to reality.

"I don't think it's going to work. We are going to need something else."

That little split-level house near the Mississippi River in Cottage Grove is our home. We love it, but how can I move around in that place with all the steps?

The mere fact that we are talking about what to do when I leave the hospital is not only good; it's fantastic. The very process of solving our housing issue is going to give us a lot to think about, other than medical treatments, for the next few months. First, we need to find the right builder and work out the plans. Katie is uneasy but I'm almost levitating with excitement at the thought of designing our new house. Those HGTV shows suddenly take on a whole new life as I contemplate designing my new house, and watching home improvement shows on television gives me something meaningful to do.

Somehow Katie keeps changing the direction of the conversation as she tells me the surgeons discovered another previously undetected broken bone at the top of my right buttock, the "pointed bone," as she calls it. Considering all of my other issues, the surgeons elect to leave it alone and allow it to continue healing on its own.

"Hello, John," a soft voice drifts through the doorway as Tom and El Porter arrive with broad smiles, plenty of conversation, and a tin of warm chocolate chip cookies. The Porters were the very first visitors, other than family and hospital staff, who we talked with shortly after leaving ICU. They visit Walter Reed every Tuesday and Thursday with fresh chocolate chip cookies and soothing words for the troops. We have grown to look forward to their visits more than just about any others. They are so easy to talk with, and they have no hidden agenda. We knew Tom was a Korean War veteran, but we didn't realize until now that he had been injured. He explains, "I was injured and today is my 54th Alive Day. That's when you celebrate the day you didn't die."

They clearly take joy from giving without asking for anything in return. Katie and I have taken a strong liking to the Porters, but we realize we don't know much about them. Katie just up and asks Tom, "How did you two meet?"

Thanking Tom and El Porter for cookies and love

Tom turns his ever-present, twinkling gaze our way and explains, "El was my physical therapy nurse after I got injured. That's why I always tell all you young guys to hold your chin up and keep smiling, because you never know who is going to walk through that door. Heck, it could be your partner for the next fifty years." He reaches around El and pulls her tightly to emphasize a love that anyone can see every time Tom and El look at one another.

"Yup, now we have adult children, grandchildren, and a whole hospital full of soldiers."

"I didn't know you were injured in Korea," I glance at Tom. "What happened?"

"Just like you, I lost my legs."

"No shit? You walk so well I never noticed that."

"Yeah, well, I do okay for an old-timer."

"Okay? You are doing great. I'm going to do it, too, just like you did. And, someday I'll come back here to show guys how it works, maybe I'll even bring some cookies."

"Hey, folks, I have a lot of cookies that need to be delivered," El interrupts. "John and Katie, we absolutely love visiting with you. Please let us know if there is anything you need other than cookies. If you aren't getting something, if there is any concern, just let us know and we'll see what can be done."

Chapter 28

A Startling Discovery

January 10, 2007

I get a strange phone call from Iraq. CPT Chip Rankin, 1LT. Wade Blomgren, and SSG Tim Nelson are all there on a speaker phone from Fallujah. I don't pick up on their somber mood, but something is definitely odd as they babble on about nothing. Little do I know that all the other phones on Camp are turned off as is the practice when there is a fatality and, as much as they want to tell me what has happened, they cannot say a word.

Moments later Master Sergeant Newcomer walks into my room accompanied by another soldier.

"Hey, what brings you to town?"

"We have to go to NGB (National Guard Bureau) to talk about Bradleys."

That's definitely weird, but in my drug-slowed state of mind that doesn't register. Oddly, the guy who had done so much for Katie and me appears uncomfortable and says he has to leave but will be back soon.

Katie needs something to eat, so she heads down to the chow hall with Master Sergeant Newcomer. Alone for a rare moment, I flip on the laptop and go to startribune.com to find out if the Minnesota Wild NHL hockey team won last night and up pops a news item: "St. Paul Soldier Killed in Iraq."

The Red Bulls have 3,800 troops in Iraq so the chance that I know this one is small, but I'm curious and click on the headline. A giant photo of my good friend Jimmy Wosika fills the screen. The computer sucks the wind from me, rips out my heart.

Jimmy died a true hero making certain his men were safe. Yesterday he was leading 1st Squad on patrol near the village of Zanti, a basically routine day that was going smoothly until they spotted one of the popular white pickup trucks sitting unattended alongside the road with the hood raised, a common sight in the dusty environment where old, poorly maintained vehicles constantly stall out.

Jimmy and SGT Jon Goldstein surveyed the empty truck through their rifle scopes. Seeing nothing abnormal, they ordered SPC Luc Moua, SPC David Steinbruckner, and Navy Corpsman Daniel "Doc" Fox to stay back while the two sergeants moved in to inspect the truck. Goldstein approached on the left while Wosika looked under the hood. Spotting nothing out of order Wosika moved to the driver's side and looked in the window just as the truck exploded.

Goldstein was approaching the right side of the vehicle and was tossed into the desert. Not seriously injured, he quickly got to his feet and joined the Squad searching for Jimmy, praying against all logic that somehow Wosika had survived. They searched through a marsh of cattails next to the canal where they found his shredded body armor and then came upon his remains, identifiable by the familiar tattoo on his back.

Woman's intuition or just overriding concern causes Katie to leave Brian in the chow hall when she thinks he is taking too long. She returns only minutes after I spot the news report to find me bawling like a starved infant.

"John, what is the matter?"

Unable to make words, I manage to point at the computer. It

punches Katie almost as hard as it hit me. She knows how close I was with Jimmy. I don't remember ever being in the Army without him. We came in about the same time, trained together, "vacationed" in Kosovo together, and fought together in Iraq. Now, he dies in a car bomb blast only a short distance from where Bryan and Corey died.

When Jimmy and I were in training at Camp Shelby, Katie sent me home-baked cookies every week. He was crazy for her oatmeal raisin cookies, said they were "the best" he had ever eaten. She started sending him a weekly batch, and I got peanut butter chocolate chips. Now, she was stunned and in pain; but for my sake she held it together while I cried and cried more than I have ever cried in my life, and hopefully more than I will ever cry again.

"Oh, no, I'm so sorry," sputters Master Sergeant Newcomer when he re-enters. "I wanted to tell you so badly, but I couldn't say anything until it was officially released."

Suddenly the strange phone call from Iraq and Newcomer's mysterious trip to Washington, D.C., to talk about nonsense comes clear. Everybody wanted to tell me what had happened, but nobody could say a word until the families were notified, and that was supposed to have happened by four p.m. Somehow the news media got the word a few minutes early and I just happened to flip on my laptop at the worst possible moment.

My room quickly fills with nurses and hospital staff. All want to help, but there is nothing anyone can do to make this pain go away. I just want to be alone.

My first thought is for my guys back in Iraq and how this is hitting them. They just had a funeral for two brothers last month and five weeks later, another one. Pain gives way to intense anger. I want to leap from this damn bed, fly back to Iraq, to exact some revenge on the cowards who did this

I met James Wosika Jr. in late 2000 when he joined the Minnesota National Guard and was assigned to my unit in East St. Paul. Jimmy and I were among a group of guys all about the same age who moved up the ranks together becoming more like brothers.

We hung out together on Guard drill events, through training, and when we were away from the Guard. Often, we got together just to talk, drink, and laugh.

Unlike civilian friends who always seem to be very high maintenance, Army buddies can go months without speaking and then get together and laugh like we never were apart. I recall in August 2005, when we were getting ready to head off to Camp Shelby for training before going to Iraq; Jimmy called and said he was coming over, he never asked, he always just said, "I'm coming over," and it seemed as natural as breathing.

He showed up with a bottle of Alize and some orange juice, and I laughed out loud. If we are going to sit here and drink, at least let's put down some Captain Morgan or some good whiskey, but not some "fruity girl drink."

Jimmy smiled, poured the Alize, and we drank his fruit juice. I could never say "no" to Jimmy. He was always just too nice. It made him such an easy target, and I couldn't resist the temptation to constantly jab him with some silly remark. He never did anything back other than shoot out his ever present "Whatever man, fuck you," and bust out that gigantic, ear-to-ear Jimmy smile.

I will never forget the reconnaissance mission in Kosovo when Rene Montero, Eng Yang, Jimmy, and I spent three days searching the woods near Serbia's border for smugglers. We didn't find any smugglers, but there was plenty of rain—three days of rain. Calling on our survival training, we dug channels to drain water away, grabbed sticks, and built lean-to shelters with our rain gear. The whole assignment sucked, but we made it fun. Everybody brought three days worth of MREs except Jimmy. He packed one MRE, a box of Cheez-Its, and a huge container of grape Kool-Aid. Every time he mixed up a batch to drink, he did the grape Kool-Aid dance until our sides hurt from laughing. Jimmy was nuts for chocolate ice cream and just about any manner of snack food.

On his MySpace Internet page, Jimmy said his heroes were "any man or woman that has died for this country." Now he is my hero. He died heroically, thinking first of his men.

Now I just can't stop thinking about my guys in Iraq. Suddenly, as if losing another brother isn't enough, President Bush picks today of all days to announce his new plan for the war in Iraq—a troop surge. He's on television to explain that the new commander in Iraq, Gen. David Petraeus, will shift

Jimmy serves up Kool-Aid, junk food, and laughs

the mission of American troops from supporting Iraqi forces to protecting the population, which involves moving into the cities and working more closely with Iraqi forces and civilians. Everyone I know feels that General Petraeus, a brilliant military strategist and former West Point professor, is the right guy. They say he knows where to find the brightest minds in the military and that he is one of those rare senior officers who does not hesitate to accept advice from low-ranking grunts or civilians. It appears that, if anyone can change the mission and make it work, Petraeus is the guy.

To support the surge, the president is sending five more brigades, thirty thousand troops, to Iraq over the next six months, bringing the total to one hundred sixty thousand troops plus one hundred sixty thousand civilian contractors (the civilians include Iraqis, Americans, and those from other countries). Then comes the shocker: until the new troops arrive, some of those already in Iraq will be extended. That turns out to include Minnesota's Red Bulls, 1-34th Brigade Combat Team including my unit, Bravo Company 2–136th. So, instead of coming home in March, my guys are put back in the field until July for the longest deployment of any unit to serve in Iraq, sixteen months, plus all the training time.

The extension sucks, but at least Bravo Company is going to get the chance to dig out the scum who have been killing our guys. Revenge is always compelling when you watch your brothers massacred. After we were hit, our guys wanted revenge; but they remained professional American soldiers. Just as in civilian life, American justice does not tolerate vigilante reprisal, especially killing innocent people; it is what separates us from insurgent terrorists. That doesn't make it any easier, but it defines who we are, what America represents to the world.

Chapter 29

HELP FROM HOME BOOSTS MY SPIRIT

Back at Walter Reed, I notch another milestone on January 15— last night I peed on my own. Please excuse my irrational exuberance but this is fantastic progress. Until now every time I had to pee, Katie had to insert the catheter, not particularly pleasant for either of us. More than that, the final stitches were removed from my left leg, and for the first time since December 2, I have no stitches. Now I need to get the feeling back in my left thumb and pointer finger.

Katie is praying that my appetite returns because I have lost so much weight. But who can eat after downing a cup full of pills three times a day. That tasty little meal takes ten to fifteen minutes each time, and the pills aren't even flavored. It reminds me of *The Jetsons,* space-age cartoons on Saturday mornings when I was a boy, describing the wonders of tomorrow where people will live on exotic pills rather than the meals. Let's hope *that* version of the future never comes.

Something incredibly wonderful happens back in Minnesota on Friday, January 19. The American Legion in Hugo hosts a fund-raiser for me and my family. It's January in Minnesota (when thermometers often tumble below zero), but that doesn't stop more than three thousand people from showing up. The crowd is so big there are times when they all can't fit in the building and some brave the savage icy wind and wait their turn for entry.

Traffic is so heavy they need police to help, and giant lighted advertising signs are scattered on the nearby highway that say, "SGT John Kriesel Benefit." Some of my buddies, Jack Buckingham, Eric Negron, Tom Forchas, and John Rowley, organized the benefit along with Marv Siedow, grandfather of a high school classmate. Siedow attacked the Twin Cities like a man possessed, as he visited nearly every business in the town with his demand for auction items. He was hugely successful.

Jack Buckingham's father, Jay, brought in the grand prize, an all-expense-paid trip to Las Vegas, donated by the Minnesota Twins. An executive with Old Dutch Foods, Jay had a strong relationship with the Twins as an advertiser at the games.

I wish we could be there, but I'm stuck in this bed. Amazingly, most of the people who come don't know me or Katie at all; they just care. We always talk about "Minnesota Nice," and now I know it truly does exist.

Just when my weight is starting to come back, much to Katie's delight, I get the flu and take another one of those steps back. I'm back eating through an IV tube in my arm. I must say the intravenous cuisine obviously is even less tasty than my three cups of pills although far simpler to digest directly in the arm. Apparently, the stomach flu is running wild through Ward 57.

The flu we can handle. What comes next is a new infection in my right leg, and I can tell from the grim look on Katie's face as the doctor describes a new treatment plan that it is something to worry about. One of the wire stitches used to attach my muscle to the bone is being rejected by my body, and that is causing the new infection. Here we go off to what seems to be a daily routine of CT scans to ensure that the infection is localized. Surgery is scheduled tomorrow to treat it. That's today's bad news.

The good news: the orthopedic doctors announce that my back is healing very well and I am able to sit up as much as I want, albeit with extreme caution. Turning in bed must be done only in the "log roll" method, which they explain means turning the entire body without twisting. Sitting up, wow! That's not good news; it's *great* news.

Things continue to improve when doctors learn the infection is localized, and they are able to clean the area and treat it with antibiotics. The treatment is successful, though the pain is brutal; but I survive and soon feel like a million bucks.

"I want to go for a ride," I announce to Katie.

Another benchmark day arrives as I ease into a wheelchair and roll down the hallway in Ward 57 to inspect the world on the other side of the doorway that has been little more than a window for nearly two months. It's amazing how a vision of normal can change. Suddenly here I am in a place where most of the guys are in wheelchairs, pushing walkers, or learning to use prosthetics, I'm not a freak; I'm just one of the guys, here. In fact, the strangers are those few people with two legs and two arms; everyone on Ward 57 is missing parts. It brings to mind a rerun on television, probably in the middle of the night when I couldn't sleep, of an old *Twilight Zone* that used some version of that theme. Normal is nothing more than whatever the majority possesses.

Virtually overnight, life has changed dramatically. Last weekend I was battling a vicious case of the flu and dreading surgery. By Wednesday I am sitting up, riding in my new chariot and cleared to eat real food—now I know this pill thing will never catch on. My hospital meals are supplemented by Katie who obviously is trying to pump up my weight. There's Dunkin' Donuts with breakfast and a twelve-inch sub and a giant chocolate chip cookie from Subway added to the regular hospital lunch.

Getting up and moving around makes a big difference in my mood, expectations, and health. Almost immediately my kidneys return to normal operation. For the first time since that horrible day of December 2, I get dressed in a T-shirt and shorts; it feels better than a new suit.

The timing couldn't be better. Elijah and Brody arrive for a "sleepover," and we acquire another "bed chair" for the room. On Thursday we're getting ready for dinner when the nurse knocks and tells us we have a visitor.

"Cool, send them in."

Singer Justin Timberlake walks in, shakes my hand, and starts talking just like a regular guy. The boys appear puzzled as they ask, "Who are you?"

"My name is Justin."

I look at the boys and explain, "He's the guy who sings 'SexyBack.'" I remember hearing it frequently on the radio in Minnesota when I was home on leave, and I know the boys like it.

"You didn't sing that song," one of them says with confidence.

He crouches down to their level and looks them straight in the eye, "I promise you that I did sing that song."

"Cool." Not a raving exclamation, just a slight smile and a soft "cool."

But, I'm very impressed with Justin. A lot of entertainers, politicians, and athletes come through the hospital with huge entourages and photographers causing a ruckus; but Justin appears alone in the evening and quietly expresses a sincere interest in me. He just sits down, hangs out, and talks. It's me who finally begs off because Katie and I are going out on our first dinner with the boys and her parents. I have had more visitors than I can count, but he is one of my favorites because, although he is a huge star with tons of money, today he is just a guy talking to me.

Operation Second Chance made plans for dinner, but as we are getting ready to go, they call and cancel due to snowy weather. Not to be denied, Katie returns to SFAC for another taxi voucher, which she obtains with less grief than before. Everything is going well until we discover that I just cannot get into the taxi. Dinner out is cancelled.

Celebrities of all shapes and sizes are regular visitors at Walter Reed almost daily. Maj. Gen. Larry Shellito, Minnesota Adjutant General, comes several times. Another favorite moment is when Minnesota Vikings wide receiver Cris Carter visits the Physical Therapy Center with another former NFL receiver, Cris Collinsworth; radio celebrity, Bob Costas; and *Sports Illustrated* writer, Peter King. Carter has a public reputation for having a difficult personality, but I love the way he plays. I want to meet him. Just as most of the stories that come out of Iraq are tainted by the news media, Carter's reported "poison" personality turns out to be a gross exaggeration. He's a great guy.

Among the others who visit are singer Jonny Lang, comedian Ron White, Gary Sinise, Caroline Rhea, actor Jeff Daniels, Secretary of Defense Robert Gates, Secretary of State Condoleezza Rice, radio host Delilah, and actors John Voight and Justin Bartha. Voight and Bartha are in town filming *National Treasure 2*, but Bartha is more interested in sharing ideas on poker, something we both love. (He became better known for his part as Doug in the movie *The Hangover*.)

It's getting to be action central with one guest after another, but I take special note when Governor Tim Pawlenty sticks his head in the door.

"Hi, Sergeant."

"Hello Governor. Thanks for coming. I've been thinking that I will need a job when I get back to Minnesota. Maybe I should run for governor." I guess it's the drugs talking, but we had a good laugh.

Actor Gary Sinise visits

We share some time with one of my all time favorite Vikings, Cris Carter

Chapter 30

Physical Therapy Begins

It's Christmas all over again in early February when I am cleared to begin physical therapy one hour, six times a week, and occupational therapy one hour, five times a week. On top of that I'm scheduled for x-rays every two weeks in search of enough improvement for my legs to be fitted for prosthetics. If nothing else, all the activity gets me up and moving. You can only watch so much daytime television. Already the muscle I have regained in therapy enables me to get myself in and out of the wheelchair.

The thrill dims slightly as I struggle mightily to meet the constantly increasing demands of the physical therapists. They focus on improving flexibility in my lower body in preparation for the day when I will be fitted for prosthetics. Meanwhile the occupational therapists work to build and refine my motor skills. They constantly push me to the limit, but Katie is right there, urging me onward. I can't disappoint her, and I know I'll never get out of here if I don't push through the pain. So, I drive that much harder day after day doing double sessions. Every time it starts to get easier they ratchet up the intensity.

The PT room is a fitness center on steroids. There is constant high energy activity going on everywhere with a couple dozen conversations, all amped up at the same time. Each soldier has his or her non-medical attendant (NMA)—better known as wife, mom, dad, sister, or brother there, voicing encouragement, massaging aching muscles, and learning the next routine. Most professional athletes don't train as much or as hard as wounded warriors.

Those who have progressed to prosthetic legs navigate back and forth across the room or, when the weather cooperates, they head outside for some realistic practice. They don't just walk or run. They navigate obstacle courses, or one of the physical therapists wraps an enormous rubber band around the soldier's waist and her own, then provides drag as the wounded warrior pulls the therapist. The rest of us climb onto padded benches where we wrestle with an unending series of equipment to strengthen muscles in preparation for the day when we will get to "run" down the hallway. Conversation is unending. Sergeant Troy, a docile black Lab that is fully outfitted with a jacket and official stripes, roams eagerly, accepting all the petting and hugs we can give. The docile PT dog is everybody's friend, just moving from person to person, giving as much love as he gets.

The most amazing feature of the PT room is the camaraderie among all of the soldiers, marines, family members, and staff. There is no rank here. Everybody helps anyone who needs assistance anytime, without hesitation. It's as though we are all in the same family, one very huge family, and in many ways I guess we are. The only break in routine comes when one of our many VIP visitors drops in, a daily parade of generals, Hollywood stars, government officials, and famous athletes, as well as plenty of politicians.

The healing process is aided immensely by the continuous flow of visitors, especially those from home like Bryan McDonough's parents and two of Jimmy Wosika's relatives. Seeing familiar faces, talking to folks back home by phone, and keeping up with everyone by e-mail definitely helps battle the stress and anxiety of not knowing what lies ahead.

Indianapolis Colts head coach Tony Dungy, running back Joseph

President Bush stops in at PT

**Indianapolis Colts owner Jim Irsay shows off
Super Bowl trophy**

Addai, offensive coordinator Tom Moore, and team owner Jim Irsay come through, carrying the 2007 Vince Lombardi Super Bowl Trophy, a regulation-sized football made of pure silver by Tiffany & Co. Like a boy, I gingerly touch the giant silver ball and, I swear, electricity shoots up my arm. I look at the proud champions with a smile and quip, "As a Vikings fan, this may be as close as I'll ever come to the Lombardi trophy."

Addai is another down-to-earth guy. He sits down for a long time and just talks about everything from his high school days to the Super Bowl. It is difficult not noticing his mammoth wristwatch with a circle of enormous diamonds flashing like a dozen cameras at a press conference. At one point Katie can't resist asking, "Do you know what time it is?"

He looks at his watch before glancing up to capture Katie's humor. We all laugh.

Irsay spots Josh Bleill, an Indiana Marine, another double amputee, who went to the Super Bowl with the Colts, and they relive the game. Bleill rubs the silver ball for good luck, although no Genie pops out, Irsay tells him, "Josh, I will promise you two things. If you want to come home, I'll fly you home and when you get there you come and see me about a job." (Bleill joined the Colts' staff in 2009 as community spokesperson.)

A band of angels from Operation Second Chance comes through February 8 to help me escape Walter Reed for the first time with Katie and a few other soldiers on a trip to a Washington Capitals hockey game. My first venture into the public domain is an incredible experience. I hardly notice the actual game, who wins, or anything about it; but dining in the luxurious Acela Club and lounging in a private suite is special.

Not so special is the taste of reality that slaps me in the face as I wheel through the crowd. For the past three months, I have been cocooned in my new "Twilight Zone" world surrounded by other amputees and injured soldiers. Suddenly here I am alone in the crowd and they are staring at me. Some smile and nod in support, a few even clap as I roll past, but it feels very uncomfortable. By God, I'm proud of my wounds. I earned them standing up for freedom.

The thrill of knocking off a big goal and escaping to the real world even for a few hours is offset the next night when my Fallujah blast explodes in a nightmare so realistic I can see, feel, and taste the dust and gun powder. I am lying on the road again with my legs in tourniquets, praying for the helicopter, expecting to die. Shaking with terror and dripping in sweat I lurch into consciousness and spot Katie sound asleep in the giant chair beside my bed. Darkness makes the nightmare that much more frightening, and I fear going back to sleep, but eventually I pass out with no more dreams.

"What's wrong, honey?" Katie inquires when she detects my state of depression the next morning.

"Don't ever do that again," she admonishes upon hearing of the nightmare. "That's why I stay here; so you won't be alone. Promise me that you will wake me anytime you need me, even just to talk."

Thinking it through, I decide that rather than startle her awake by yelling in the middle of the night I will use the dainty little round blue sponge on a stick that resembles something mom would use to clean toilets to tap Katie gently until she awakes. The sponge on a stick actually was given to me to tease my stumps in order to eliminate nerve sensitivity, but it proves more useful for tapping Katie.

We're settling into our routine once more, if routine is a word in the recovery dictionary, when the girlfriend of another wounded warrior from down the hall approaches Katie to ask if she could keep an eye on her boyfriend until his parents arrive. The girlfriend needs to get back to college for finals, and the guy's parents can't make it here for a couple days. Reluctantly, Katie agrees. What are the options? Slipping into the room, she finds the guy with two legs amputated above the knees and a tracheotomy in his throat, making conversation a one-sided event. She does her best, holding his hand, asking, "Do you need anything. Are you lonely?" But, he can't respond.

She comes back crying like a baby. "John, I can't do this. I can deal with our problems. I'm coping; but I can't take on other people's sadness. It's going to crush me. I feel we have some control over our situation, but I look at these other people, and it's the saddest thing I have ever seen. I can't help them." In spite of her pain, Katie checks on him constantly until his family arrives.

Without doubt my most exciting day since arriving at Walter Reed is February 14, Valentine's Day. I break out of the building for dinner with Katie at Ruth's Chris Steakhouse, our favorite place to dine. Somehow the Minnesota Chapter of the Patriot Guard discovered that I wanted to take Katie to our favorite restaurant; so, they arranged for dinner and picked up the tab. Operation Second Chance provided transportation and sent along a dozen roses that I requested for Katie with a note reading, "Happy Valentine's Day to my favorite Nurse."

The weather is crappy, spitting a couple inches of wet snow that nearly shuts down the Capital City. Apparently, their answer to snow is: Why waste money plowing when it is bound to melt eventually? Riding through town, we witness the most pathetic display of winter driving we have ever seen. But, hey, we're from Minnesota; this is nothing. Dinner is fabulous, and I put down the biggest meal I've eaten in months followed by a drive through downtown Washington, D.C., for my first ever look at the National Mall, Lincoln Memorial, Vietnam Memorial, and all of the other incredible historic sites. The sight is magnificent with lights twinkling across the newly fallen snow crystals. It's a magical scene with the nation's core silenced beneath a blanket of pure white.

Chapter 31

THERAPEUTIC CUDDLING

There are times when I wish I were still in my eight-day coma, especially at night when I drift back to the desert, bleeding and broken, terrified that I am about to die. The nightmares are relentless, ripping away any comfort I manage to achieve. No drug is powerful enough to push them away.

Katie sleeps in the chair beside me and suffers almost as much, maybe more, with every fire team command I bark out, shattering the night air on my visits to the desert and the constant fight to survive, over and over. One night the dream is so vivid I rip out my Leatherman knife, sit up in bed and scan the room still half-asleep.

"John, what are you doing?" Katie interrupts.

"Clearing the room."

"The room is clear," she reports in a calm tone.

"Roger," I reply and fall back asleep totally oblivious to the entire incident.

In desperation, after watching me fight off invisible insurgents for several nights, Katie climbs into bed with me and I fall fast asleep like a newborn. She does it again the next night, and the next. It works like a charm, no bad dreams whatsoever. Then a new nurse appears on the scene, roaring at Katie to "get out of that bed. You can't do that here; get out of the bed."

Startled awake, I unleash a violent tirade and order her to get the hell out of my room. She exits quickly.

Next day we reveal Katie's miraculous nightmare cure to Dr. Janze. He immediately goes to the hospital computer to write the very first "therapeutic cuddling" order in the history of Walter Reed Army Medical Center, and Dr. Goff signs off on it as well. Occasionally a new nurse stumbles into the room in shock to find Katie sleeping by my side, only to disappear after being directed by Katie to check the orders in the computer.

I was never much of a video game nut, but Dr. Janze suggests that playing video games might be good physical therapy for my hands. My left hand is numb near the thumb and pointer finger and doesn't want to take orders from my brain. So, when a couple of friends from home arrive with an Xbox 360 I start challenging anybody who dares to enter my room. It isn't long before both arms are working well and I am becoming a master video competitor.

In addition to patching all my physical holes, the Army is worried about my head. Some wounded warriors have problems dealing with injuries; many of them dig deep in depression with the "why me" puzzle. Thankfully, I don't have that problem, but Walter Reed keeps sending a psychiatrist to examine me. He verbally pokes and prods my brain, looking for damage, but I keep telling him that I am okay.

"Not really," he says. "This will take time."

I understand all that. It is going to take some time. That's not the problem. He's the problem, with his aggressive interrogation and constant challenges to my answers. The guy drives me nuts. I understand that he needs to do this and that I may need some help, but this guy really annoys me. My blood pressure shoots off the chart every time he walks in my room. Dr. Janze arrives and tells me they have many psychiatrists and he will find another one. He brings in Dr. Andrea Bouterie who proves to be kind, compassionate, and easy to talk to.

Chapter 32

A Trip to the White House, Almost

My body is actually beginning to improve to the point that I'm two weeks ahead of schedule to start walking. Katie notifies the White House that I am ready to accept the chief of staff's offer to visit, and the date is set for Saturday, February 24.

Nancy Matthews and Lea Dale, another friend of Katie's from work, fly into town for my big day, and my brother, Dave, and Dr. Janze plan to join us. Friday night Katie's friends invite us to dinner, but I beg off just to be cautious due to a slight stomach ache, probably the flu. I don't want to do anything to jeopardize my trip to the White House. I settle for dinner from Subway and launch into a serious Xbox battle with Dave, but the stomach ache just gets worse.

Katie doesn't make it back until almost two a.m., and she's pretty happy, although her medication of choice is margaritas. Nancy and Lea hauled her off to a hole-in-the-wall Mexican joint for a spicy dinner and margaritas by the pitcher. Existing on Girl Scout cookies and water with an occasional trip to Subway for two months gave way to a night of fun and margaritas. Following dinner it was like a slumber party with three high school girls letting loose, laughing, and talking about every silly thing they could think about until the waiter explained it was nearly midnight.

Outside they discovered that their parking ramp closed at eleven p.m. and no one was there to retrieve their car. Someone finally answered their frantic plea on the emergency phone line, but they waited outside in one of Washington's less desirable neighborhoods for nearly an hour.

She arrives at the hospital to find me still not feeling well, but we convince each other that it must be a recurrence of the flu and fall asleep. An hour later I'm throwing up over the side of the bed and we both bolt awake. By morning there is no doubt that this is more than the flu when I try to get ready, but vomit again and lose consciousness. Katie calls the White House to cancel and notifies Dr. Janze who asks for my symptoms. It's his day off, but he appears in minutes. A quick check of my colostomy bag and he realizes I haven't gone to the bathroom recently.

"We need to get you down for a CT scan immediately," he says. "I'm thinking that you have a small bowel obstruction."

"No, I'm fine. It's just the flu," I reply, not wanting to go through that again.

"No, it's not. We need to deal with this right now."

The CT scan proves him right again. Scar tissue from intestinal surgery is blocking my small intestine, and the bowel is in immediate danger of exploding. Wonderful, now I am building an IED right inside my gut. As if things aren't bad enough, the crowd of doctors and nurses in my room starts arguing over treatment. I have been on a blood thinner, and that makes surgery an extreme risk at the same time that the bomb in my intestines is growing by the minute. I can't believe that I lived through losing two legs and all of the other trauma and I'm about to die because I can't crap.

As I waver in and out of consciousness, a nurse is stuffing an NG tube up my nose and down to my intestines to suck waste from my stomach. It is incredibly nasty, one of the most uncomfortable procedures you can imagine; and I've had plenty of experience to compare against it. My eyes flicker open, and there's Katie in panic with Nancy and Lea doing their best to keep her calm while the crowd of nurses is freaking out. I'm thinking this is not good. They hold off thirteen hours for the blood thinner to clear my body and rush me into surgery.

Doctor Janze says medical students are taught "never let the sun set on a small bowel obstruction" because it can be fatal if not particularly poetic, but he makes the point. When I come down off the anesthesia, I'm not so sure I care about surviving as intense pain sinks its vicious talons into my gut. To access my stomach and intestines, they had cut along the previous scar line, there is no more painful part of the body to slice; I just wish I wasn't becoming such an expert on pain.

I log another eleven hours in the surgical intensive care unit (SICU) while they struggle to manage my pain. Room 5735 has been home for two months, and suddenly they are saying that we will be in another room once I got out of SICU. It's home and I don't want another room. So, I suck it up and they move us back to Ward 57. Pain is so intense that I don't even make it through a full nursing shift before they drag me back to SICU early Monday for another four days. At least they agree to keep my room.

Pain isn't the only obstacle in SICU; boredom takes a toll. Although we have a television, computers, cell phones, and anything else that might take my mind off the pain are banned. Katie tries to keep everyone up-to-date, but the cell phone ban is driving her crazy. At first she drops down to another floor. Finally she decides to just go down the hall where she gets scolded. Already upset, she walks into my room and a nurse tells her, "There's no way he can be in that much pain. We're giving him enough Ketamine to put down an elephant."

"Well, take a look at the skinny little guy lying there in pain," Katie reacts. "Whatever you're doing is not working. I don't care if it's enough to put down an elephant; it's not working. So, you are not helping me right now. You're just pissing me off."

At that point Katie goes into a meltdown, thinking to herself, *It's never going to end. I'm never getting out of here. He's never going to get better. I can't do this anymore. It's always something, and there's nothing I can do to fix him.*

She's incredibly strong and, up to this point, has hidden her grief from me, but falling back into the intensive care unit after two months is almost more than either one of us can handle. Luckily, her crisis passes quickly, and she is back to normal two days later when the doctors finally get my pain under control.

It is such a major event when I finally return to Ward 57, some of the nurses are cheering, clapping, and welcoming me home like a miniature New York ticker tape parade, except that there is no tickertape or confetti falling from the windows. I have never been so happy to be anywhere as to be home in Ward 57, Room 35.

The human body is an amazing machine, defending itself against all manner of attack. In this case my intestines shut down in reaction to trauma from the surgery, a normal occurrence anytime the intestines feel threatened. Doctor Koo explains that it is nothing to worry about other than the temporary need for another NBO order (nothing by oral). I'm back sipping the damp sponge, longing for anything to eat—I fantasize over a trip downstairs to Subway.

Doctors and nurses are constantly listening to my stomach for any hint of activity and hand me a stethoscope to search for sound, but a week passes in silence. Then one morning a woeful moan erupts from my belly and I want to scream with joy at the sound of that sweet rumble. I'll never again be embarrassed if my stomach speaks up in public.

Chapter 33

DOES CAMERA INSURANCE COVER AN IED BLAST?

A wave of good karma comes through the door as Dr. Janze announces that my damaged intestines have responded well enough to enable removal of that horrible NG tube from my nose. I hope never to see another nose hose. Best of all, I am able to take a few sips of water for the first time in two weeks. Sips may not sound like much, but they slide down my parched throat smoother than ice cream in the desert. Chalk off another goal accomplished, or is that re-accomplished.

Three days later, it gets even better when I am cleared to take on solid food, and I savor every bite. The day turns Olympic gold when I am fitted for my prosthetic legs, truly the beginning of my return to life. Just when I think this day can't possibly get any better, Katie's parents walk into my room with Elijah and Brody.

The casting process for my prosthetic legs is pretty interesting. First they wrap my stumps with a type of Ace bandage soaked in plaster. Once the bandages dry, the prosthetics team pulls them off and fills the "negative" space with a different variety of plaster that will not stick to the cast. They create an exact replica of each leg, the "positive," for use in building my prosthetic sockets. Over the next two days, they work to craft a perfect fit so that all my weight will rest comfortably into the prosthetics.

Katie is with me for the fitting, and I am so high on anticipation I could almost walk on air without any mechanical devices. As so often happens in the healing process, this is another false alarm: the sockets don't fit properly. Although disappointing, they say this is not uncommon. In fact, the sockets are made of thick plastic and purposely oversized so that they can be adapted to the leg—a very slow, exacting process.

So, I have to spend another weekend bound to the wheelchair; though I must say, Nancy and Lea brought along what must be the finest wheelchair on earth. It's a power assist chair, which means that it works like a manual wheelchair except that it has a battery and small motor in each wheel so that when you thrust yourself forward power kicks in and you go three times as far as you would with the same amount of energy in a standard, manual wheelchair. The chair is extra special because Lea's husband customized it like a luxury car, painting it Minnesota Vikings purple complete with my favorite team's logo.

Determined not to let disappointment spoil a weekend with the boys and her parents, Katie and I leave the hospital for a trip to the National Air and Space Museum. Just getting out of the hospital, away from the IV tubes for a few hours, is exhilarating.

We stop at Circuit City where I must look like the proverbial kid in a toy shop, wheeling through the aisles, taking in every amazing, new electronic marvel that has appeared while I was at war. What I really need is a new digital camera. The one Katie gave me just before I deployed to Iraq doesn't work after the IED blast, although it looks fairly unscathed except for a small dent and a hairline crack. Luckily, we had the upgraded insurance plan that goes beyond "normal wear and tear and accidents," but we wonder how far beyond the plan will go.

"So how was your camera damaged," the young woman asks without looking up.

"I was riding in a Humvee in Iraq when we hit a roadside bomb and got blown up."

"What?" Her neck almost snaps as she leaps to her feet and looks me in the eyes for the first time. "Okay, you get a new camera." Just like that she hands me a gift card for full value. We find a model one step up from the original that is actually sixty dollars cheaper, enough to pay for our trip to the museum. (I loved Circuit City and appreciated their good service; it was a sad day when they went out of business.)

As for the Museum, there is plenty to see and just watching the boys' faces light up with each new discovery is worth the trip, but getting up close and personal with the public is something less than pleasant. Suddenly, it really hits me that my life has changed forever. People are staring at me like I'm one of the exhibits, a freak. Others pretend they don't see me at all as they rudely cut right in front of me or treat me like a piece of furniture. Mostly, I ache to be independent, normal, ambulatory. I know it will get better for me, but I can't help thinking what a crime it is that people who are bound to their wheelchairs need to deal with this all their lives, and I am even more committed to walk on my own. It is a low moment. Fortunately, I am a really positive guy and don't hit bottom too often. But when I do, it is a deep, dark hole that I tumble into.

I am feeling better the next morning until I realize the boys are about to head back to Minnesota. Separation is almost unbearable, but obviously, they need some semblance of a normal life with school, sports, friends, and the rest. They visit once a month, and we decide to try for twice a month even if it will be expensive. At least this time they got a free trip when a new veterans assistance group headquartered in Minnesota sought us out. Walt Fricke and his Veterans Airlift Command, a nonprofit organization that finds private aircraft owners to provide free trips for wounded soldiers and their families, arranged for Polaris, the snowmobile people, to fly my in-laws and the boys to Washington, D.C., and back.

Chapter 34

GOAL NUMBER ONE

Talk about goals, I hit the top of the list March 16 when I wheel down to the Prosthetics Department proudly wearing a stars and stripes T-shirt, and they slip on my custom-made, high-tech legs. Initially, they feel pretty uncomfortable, but as soon as I am upright the world shifts back into alignment. Life is good.

I shuffle back and forth for hours between the parallel bars. It's weird to stand up on my new legs. Walking on these things definitely is not like climbing back on a bicycle after you fall down. This is something new, starting all over. Initially, it feels something like walking on stilts. I am clumsy and stagger along the bars, determined that nothing can stop me. Within minutes my right leg begins to feel almost like a real leg. The fact that I still have a knee and six inches of leg below it helps.

My doctor had worried that the fused pelvis and spine would limit mobility, but it feels wonderful. My gait is fairly smooth although there is a noticeable dip. Just to stand up, look people in the eyes, kiss Katie—it just doesn't get any better than this.

My left side is more challenging with that leg ending above the knee. The $40,000 prosthetic includes a mechanical knee with a miniature computer that reads data fifty times per second, sensing and adjusting to changing terrain. That's almost better than the real legs. The little computer in my new knee is programmed for my weight and the pressure required. My amazing new limb is called a C-Leg and it definitely gives new meaning to getting your "sea legs." Okay, that probably works better in audio than in print, but my first steps are pretty much the drunken-sailor gait.

I'm wondering what the "C" stands for only to learn it's nothing more than an abbreviation for 3C100, model number of the original version created by Otto Bock Healthcare Company in Germany based on an idea from Kelly James, a Canadian engineer.

The microprocessor in my bionic knee continually analyzes pressure, angle, gait, weight, and other factors, while giving instructions to a powerful hydraulic cylinder in a fraction of a second. The C-Leg navigates uneven terrain and climbs stairs. They tell me the only real downside is that my new leg doesn't like water. So I guess swimming and dancing in the rain are out. Power is provided by a forty-five-hour capacity lithium-ion battery concealed below the knee. It has a charging port just like my digital camera. There's even a twelve-volt cigarette lighter charger for the car.

The C-Leg walked into the United States in 1999 to meet growing demand for missing legs followed by constant research, refinement, and new models of ever more realistic legs and arms. Walter Reed is one of the major laboratories for developing and testing of all leg and arm prosthetics.

With my new legs secure, my prosthetist shadows me back and forth along the parallel bars, adjusting sensitivity in the knee and tweaking it constantly until I get the feel of making the bionic left knee bend. First impression, this thing is very heavy, maybe that's what happens when you load a computer into your leg.

"Lead with your right," he instructs. "That will feel the most normal and you have more control over it. You'll figure out the left leg in time."

I swing the right leg forward triumphantly, shift my weight, launch the left leg, striking the floor heel first, and rock from heel to toe, activating the microprocessor that bends my knee. It only takes a few awkward trips back and forth along the parallel bars, and I'm starting to get the hang of this. I'm ready to walk home to Minnesota right now, but I guess that will wait. Long journeys start with the first step, as they say, and I have just taken the big one.

No doubt learning to walk is easier the first time for a baby than this is for me. There's nothing natural about this process. I concentrate on putting one foot in front of the other, learning how to balance on these strange devices, determining the right length of stride, and developing the proper posture. Sitting in a wheelchair for months didn't prepare me for this, but I have a lot of help. Now I know I can do it. It's just going to take a lot of work.

You cannot imagine how exhilarating it feels to be walking after being told it might never happen. But, I still have no idea how much walking I will be able to do, and I'm not about to stop until suddenly they start turning off the lights. It's quitting time for the prosthetics staff and quitting time for me. But, at that moment, I realize that I

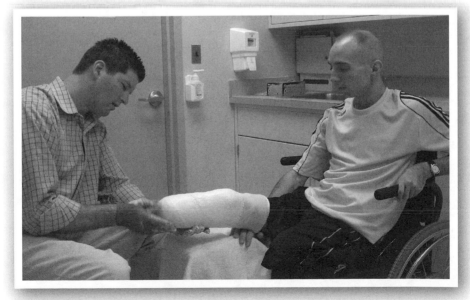

Art Molnar, one of my prosthetics specialists, fits me for my new legs

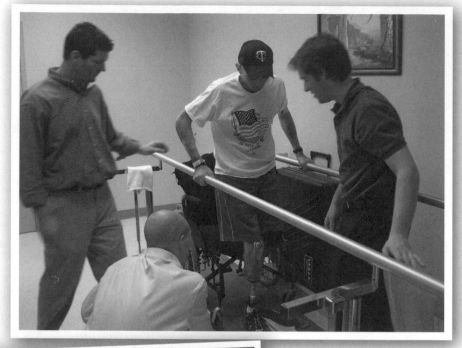

Art Molnar and Tom O'Doherty offer advice while Dr. Kyle Potter checks my first baby steps

Okay, here goes my first steps

am going to stand up and walk again without parallel bars, without canes—just stand up and walk.

Unfortunately, overdoing physical activity extracts a cost and by morning my stumps are red, throbbing, and swollen. Maybe pacing myself a bit is not such a bad idea. The swelling prevents me from wearing the prosthetics for a couple days, but I push on in PT constantly building strength until my stumps recover and I return to the parallel bars. After five days between the bars, CPT Marilyn Rodgers says I am ready for a walker. Two weeks later I toss the walker for two canes. Goal Number One accomplished—I'm up and walking.

Chapter 35

PUSHED OUT OF THE NEST

In early April, Dr. Janze announces that it's time to leave the nest. As much as I looked forward to getting out on my own, the sudden realization that I will be away from the comfort of my safety net is numbing. What if I have another bowel obstruction? How about intense pain? Could I start bleeding? Will I remember to take my pills at the right time? How fast can infection develop?

Before we head out, I start hoarding medications and medical supplies just in case something happens and we can't get back to the hospital. Katie thinks I'm crazy. She gets annoyed when I pile boxes of medical supplies on the wheelchair as she pushes me out the door and up the hill to Fisher House.

It isn't like we're being completely tossed out the door; in fact, Fisher House is still on the Walter Reed Campus, only two blocks away. It's a small building set up just for recovering soldiers and their families. We call it our apartment, but it's just one small room and a bathroom. We are barely settled in when public outcry over alleged shoddy conditions at Walter Reed rattle the administrative offices and suddenly workers are switching out our standard television set for a new Westinghouse thirty-two-inch HDTV with a DVD player, setting up a new IMac computer, and delivering a very nice, new bed. We were just fine with the original equipment, but the upgrades are definitely appreciated. I quickly set up Xbox on the HDTV, and my games come to life with realistic images.

Fisher House is designed with an ulterior motive—force everyone to mix and mingle by making the kitchen, dining area, living room, and library into common areas. Everyone is in the same boat, recovering from significant injury or illness. So, along with our nonmedical attendants, we quickly melt into this functioning frat house. We are having such a good time and everyone is so pleasant that we almost forget our hardships. I guess that's the plan.

We're still on campus with a case manager and daily physical therapy sessions, even if it is a wheelchair ride down the street to the hospital rather than merely sliding into the elevator. Wheeling to the hospital itself is pretty good exercise, at least for my arms, although it would be nice if they could find a way to eliminate that one mean hill—it's downhill to the hospital, but a steep uphill climb back at the end of a strenuous PT session.

For the trip to the hospital, I take an energy drink and a high-calorie granola bar, and slip on a pair of leather gloves, my braking system for the downhill ride. As I roll along the two-block route, it's a strange paradox that, while doctors, nurses, soldiers, and visitors are darting about at a feverish pace, I find myself slowing down, focusing on the little things that I missed while I was in Iraq and couldn't see from my hospital room. Just taking the time to appreciate the flowers, the emerald green grass, and a pesky squirrel is calming. Soaking in the warmth of a sunny day in the peaceful, well-landscaped confines of the hospital property casts a hypnotic spell in the midst of intense commotion.

My route to Walter Reed culminates with a roll past seven large, white pillars that denote the "Seven Army Values" of loyalty, duty, respect, selfless service, honor, integrity, and personal courage. As corny as we thought the values were back in basic training, they definitely have become my values and I pay them note every day—

and to catch my breath before moving inside for another grueling PT session.

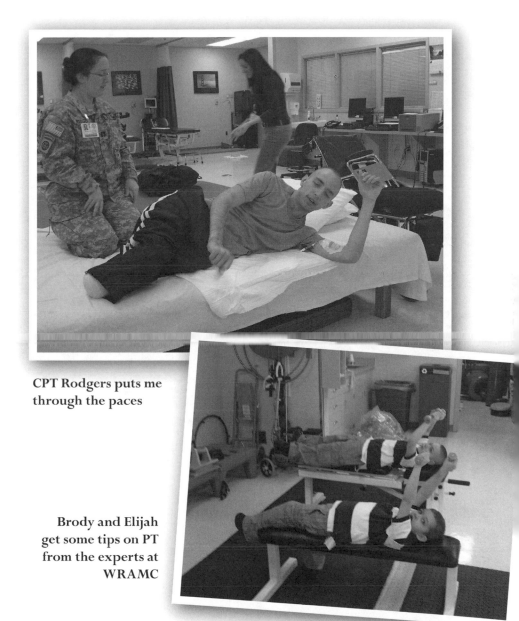

CPT Rodgers puts me through the paces

Brody and Elijah get some tips on PT from the experts at WRAMC

Chatting with Governor Tim Pawlenty at O'Gara's

Chapter 36

HOME TO MINNESOTA

Veterans Airlift Command comes through again April 23 with a ride back to Minnesota for a whirlwind series of news media interviews, public appearances, a big fund-raiser at O'Gara's Bar & Grill, a chance to throw out the first pitch at a Minnesota Twins game, and some real family time.

On the flight home, we share stories with Captains Brian R. Barber and Tim Howard, who donated their time along with the donations by Polaris and Executive Aviation. Sitting forward on the plane is a special thrill that enables me to survey the Minneapolis landscape as we drop down on Flying Cloud Airport in Eden Prairie, twenty miles south of Minneapolis. They check with the control tower and make a quick pass, rocking the plane as a wave to my boys waiting below. What an incredible day.

KARE-TV's Joe Fryer, who has done a good job telling my story in a series of television shows, meets the plane when we arrive, but we hold off the other media folks until May 4. I start the day on KFAN radio with former Minnesota Vikings player Mike Morris, Chris Hawkey, and Cory Cove for the Power Trip Morning Show, talking for an hour about my experiences in Iraq and at Walter Reed.

Katie and I settle in at Wildwood Lodge Hotel in Lake Elmo with the boys and finally slow down long enough to just be a family. I would much rather just check into our house in Cottage Grove, but it's too difficult navigating the stairs; so, this will do. It's not much like a home without a kitchen or living room, it's just a place to stay, but at least we are all together and not in a hospital.

During our stay we have use of a Dodge van from RollX Vans, a Shakopee, Minnesota, company. They met us on arrival at Flying Cloud Airport with the fully accessible vehicle that boasts a sign saying, "Wounded Warrior."

Katie starts out as chauffeur, but once inside the van I want to drive. Hand controls are attached to the gas and brake pedals, but driving a car with your hands is about like tossing a bowling ball with your feet. It's going to take a lot of practice. There are no cars in the back end of the hotel parking lot; so, I figure I might as well learn now. Easing forward I instinctively push down on the gas pedal with my right foot at the same time I am trying to work the hand controls. The van jerks and bumps along across the parking lot.

"What are you doing?" Katie says with a startled voice.

"Geez, Dad," the boys are more laughing than scared.

It suddenly occurs to me that my right leg still has a knee and the prosthetic leg works just fine, flexing and applying proper pressure to the gas pedal and brake. I scrap the hand controls and take a few spins around the parking lot like nothing ever happened—driving is just like it always has been. I'm a good driver. I love to drive.

Saturday morning I do another interview with KARE 11, this time with sports guy Eric Perkins.

Staying with the sports theme, we head to the Hubert Humphrey Metrodome in downtown Minneapolis where I have been invited to toss out the first pitch at the Minnesota Twins game. Twins public relations guy Patrick Klinger offered up the invitation at Walter Reed when he visited me along with Maj. Gen. Larry Shellito, Minnesota National Guard adjutant general, and a reporter from *Fox Sports Net* on March 14. At the time of the invitation, Klinger said the Twins wanted to honor me before a game. He asked if I would be physically able to throw out the first pitch. I wasn't sure if I could do it, but there was no way I was going to pass up the chance. "Yes, I can do it."

Before CPT Rodgers departed Walter Reed, she had time to warm up my pitching arm. She moved my PT sessions onto the hospital lawn where Sergeant Troy, the black Labrador mascot from physical therapy, had almost as much fun as me fetching and returning the ball like a true hunter.

At the Twins game more than two hundred friends and family show up, but we only have seating in the suite for twenty people; so, other than our parents and some special guests, most of my buddies are in the bleachers. Somebody props the door to the suite open with a big "Welcome to Twins Territory, SGT John Kriesel" sign in the hallway and the place is constantly overflowing with a river of people coming and going.

It's a struggle just getting around in the Metrodome. I brought along two canes, and Master Sergeant Newcomer is never far away with my wheelchair, just in case. I'm still learning how to walk. Aside from perfecting my technique, there's plenty of pain and the more I walk the more it hurts, but the crowd gives me energy and blocks much of the pain. Down on the playing field for the first pitch ceremony, the Twins provide a chair for me to wait for my big moment and then give me a ride off the field in the team's golf cart.

Rolling around the edge of the playing field we spot a giant, handmade sign draped over the stands reading: "Circle Me Bert—Kriesel's Crew" and head over to shake hands with a big pack of my buddies and their families including Justin Geslin (Goose), Andy Fraley, Jesse Glassmann, and Joe Scavo, who served with me in Kosovo.

At Twins games anyone who wants to get on television waves a "Circle Me Bert" sign hoping to catch the eye of sports announcer Bert Blyleven who will comply by drawing a circle around the sign wavers on his teleprompter. They were successful. Blyleven is a wildly popular former Twins pitcher whose credentials exceed many Hall of Fame pitchers—he deserves election into the Hall.

Gardenhire hands me the ball and a kind word

American League MVP Joe Mauer gives out some batting tips

Tossing first pitch to Manager Ron Gardenhire

My super fans filled
the outfield stands

Joe Mauer and Justin Morneau, two of the nicest guys on earth who
just happen to be incredible athletes take time to talk, and they even
listened to Brody and Elijah talk about their baseball game.

I didn't get circled, but I did get on the television broadcast
with Bert Blyleven and Dick Bremer

The guys are so excited about the chance to land on television I decide not to tell them I'm scheduled to go up into the television booth with Blyleven and announcer Dick Bremer for some friendly on-air chatter during the seventh inning.

The regular seating section is packed with friends, including some who helped organize the Hugo American Legion fund-raiser— Jack Buckingham, Tom Forchas, Eric Negron, and others. Two very special guests are Buckingham's parents, Jay and Alysia, who were my second family when I was growing up. Jay Buckingham, an executive with Old Dutch Foods, frequently took me along on family trips to see the University of Minnesota Gophers, Twins, Vikings, and other activities. I love Jack's parents.

Sunday is an unbelievable day. The St. Paul City Council has declared May 6, 2007, "SSG John Kriesel Day" and hundreds of family, friends, and total strangers show up at O'Gara's Bar & Grill for my "Life is Good" benefit. Eagle Global Logistics, organizers of the event, sold three thousand tickets to help us raise money for a new house.

Walking is a challenge, and the steps to the stage set up in O'Gara's parking lot might as well be Mt. Everest until Master Sergeant Newcomer pops up to boost me up the mountain. Minnesota Governor Tim Pawlenty introduces me to the crowd with a quip about being worried that I am coming back to take his job, another reflection on the joke I made when I first spoke with him.

"I'm a lucky guy in many, many ways," I tell those in attendance. "I will never look at any day the same again as long as I live. Each day I get to tuck my kids into bed and kiss them goodnight, and to kiss my wife goodnight. That is a gift!"

My luck even brings good weather, which is fortunate considering that the event is set up in O'Gara's parking lot and spills into the street with television trucks and news cruisers everywhere. It's humbling to think all these people are here for me. I make certain they realize that this day is for Bryan, Corey, and Jimmy—the real heroes.

Katie works her way through
the massive crowd at O'Gara's

It's SSG John Kriesel Day
In St. Paul and a great day
to be alive

Patriot Guard added plenty of color and crowd control

We have some pretty fine music with G. B. Leighton, Uncle Chunk, and Martin Zellar, and more food, beer, and prizes than one could imagine. It's an incredible party with scores of people I have not seen for years, and hundreds of strangers who just became good friends.

By Monday my stumps are throbbing, I'm exhausted, and the HO bone growth is on fire much like infection without the bacteria. But the biggest event of the week is at hand. Of all the activities and excitement for my homecoming, nothing can top when Katie and I meet with home builders Bill and Ron Derrick, Rev. Henry Williams (our pastor at Five Oaks Church in Woodbury), and a small crowd of other friends and family at our vacant lot in Cottage Grove where we bust out the shovels to break ground for a new wheelchair accessible custom home.

We bought our current house while I was in Iraq, but a split level dwelling obviously wasn't going to work. Once word got out that we wanted to build a new home, we were overwhelmed by an amazing flood of people offering to help, calling from everywhere with deals and gifts. At the time we had our hands full just keeping up with my PT regimen; so, Katie's parents took over the task of finding our best option for a house. They focused on getting us the best price.

One thing we knew for certain was that we wanted to stay in Cottage Grove, and when we found an empty lot for sale near our current home we quickly put down a deposit. Offers continued to arrive fast and furious from many kind people, and that got me planning our dream—all those days lying in bed watching HGTV and the Learning Channel were going to pay off.

When we couldn't find what we wanted among all the offers Katie's parents had picked, mostly because they were not in Cottage Grove, God moved in. A letter arrived at Walter Reed from Jeannie Derrick, who attends our church, Five Oaks Church, stating that her husband was a builder who will build us a high-quality custom home at cost. Jeannie said she had tried to contact us but had been unsuccessful. She added that she understood that we were working with another builder, but Derrick wanted to know if there was anything they could do to help. I looked at Katie, "Did you ever hear about this?"

We quickly pulled up the Derrick Custom Homes website on the computer, and we were blown away by the high quality. "Holy cow, that's perfect," I told Katie. "Give me the phone. I'm going to call her right now."

It turns out that Katie's parents had talked with Derrick, and they had explained that we already had purchased a lot from another builder. Unfortunately, that other builder offered a limited range of standard designs with no accommodations for a handicapped accessible home. Change orders were going to be difficult and costly. We quickly realized we would be better off working with Derrick Homes even if it meant losing the deposit on our land.

"John, I can't do it for free, but I will build you a Derrick Custom Home at my cost," Bill Derrick called back. "I promise you it will be the very best deal you can get."

"Absolutely," I replied before he could withdraw the offer. "I would be honored to live in a house like that."

We were thrilled at the thought of having a Derrick Custom Home, an unbelievably nice house. We started the process. I was pleased to pay part of the cost so that I could comfortably ask for the special features I want in our home.

The only glitch arose when Bill realized we really wanted to stay in Cottage Grove. After a brief search, Bill and Ron found a suitable lot but it was in a development owned by a competitor, Custom One Homes. Ron explained the situation and negotiated an agreement with Custom One Homes owner Mike Rygh to enable us to purchase the lot for Derrick to build our house. Not only did Rygh agree to the land deal, but he partnered on construction with each of the builders providing workers and subcontractors. Once again, people I don't even know step up for me and my family.

As if the weekend isn't enough excitement for my first adventure outside Washington, D.C., we head off to Jacksonville, Florida, where we are met by R.J. Meade of the Wounded Warrior Project, who made arrangements for us to be guests of the PGA Tour for the Players Championship at Sawgrass Country Club in Ponte Vedra Beach. Karen and Tom Perry are our hosts for the tournament, and they introduce us to PGA Tour golfer, Frank Lickliter II, a vigorous supporter of wounded warriors. The trip was arranged by David Pillsbury, president of PGA Tour Golf Course Properties, during a visit to Walter Reed.

That night goosebumps get even bigger when Katie and I join a gathering in the Sawgrass boardroom with all the tournament employees and players, and we're totally blown away when PGA Commissioner Tim Finchem asks us to stand. He hands us a package and announces, "John, the PGA thanks you for your service, and we are giving you and your wife lifetime honorary memberships to the TPC Twin Cities." We're nearly speechless, completely shocked.

"Are you kidding? You don't need to thank us."

On the first day of practice rounds, Frank drags me along and introduces me to fellow golfer Fred Funk. It's a bit surreal as we tag along with Frank on the first round of play. Pretty much everybody else joins the massive mobs engulfing Tiger Woods and Phil Mickelson, but we are among the few following Lickliter as he bags par and makes the cut.

Even when he's doing well, Lickliter rarely sees a television camera because an athlete who smokes is off limits to the cameras— it's almost impossible to find Frank without a wet cigarette hanging off his lip whether he's driving, putting, or just chatting. After the round he invites me to accompany him and Ernie Els into the clubhouse to watch them officially sign their scorecards. He finishes the tournament at even par, good for a tie at 37th place and a prize of $38,000. Mickelson wins.

After the tournament Licklighter invites us to his house. Every other word out of Frank's mouth is "bubba" as he shows us around his mansion nestled just off a fairway on the alternate course at Sawgrass. Furs, mounted animal heads, and wildlife rugs attest to his other passion, big-game hunting.

Monday we're back at Walter Reed, convinced that there really is life after the blast.

Suddenly it is as though the earth has shifted; for the first time I fully realize that I can function in society. Walter Reed is set up for amputees, and I feel safe here, but you can't live your life here, although some guys give up and try that. Going home is why I worked double sessions in physical therapy and did everything I could to get in shape, mentally and physically, as fast as possible. Until today I was never really certain I could do it. No matter what, there is still fear in the back of my mind. I see it in the eyes and hear it stuck in the throat of every guy here.

Am I doing the right thing?

Am I going to be able to get around?

Will I ever be normal again?

How are people going to look at me?

People tell us that the public attitude toward military veterans is much better than in the past, but I can't ignore the stories some of the older guys told about coming back from Vietnam and being spit on, cursed, and labeled baby-killers. They were young guys, just like us, doing what their country ordered them to do.

All those people in Minnesota who showed up at O'Gara's and the Twins game have no idea what they did for me and for every soldier in Minnesota. I was astounded just meeting people who supported us with sincere statements: "We've got your back. Thanks for your service." We could feel the unconditional love from friends and total strangers every minute. Just knowing how people felt convinced me Minnesota is better for me than Washington, D.C., and I have to work even harder to get back here as fast as possible.

More than that, the whirlwind of activities jammed into a week in Minnesota and Florida demonstrated clearly that the list of things

I cannot do is very small compared to the list of things I can do. I may be one of only a handful of people missing both legs, among more than five million living in Minnesota, but now I know for certain that there's not very much in a day where I have to alter what I do—maybe, sometimes, how I do it, but not what I actually do. I can function in society.

Chapter 37

SOMETIMES NORMAL ISN'T SO NORMAL

On our return to Walter Reed, we discover that my pitching coach, physical therapist CPT Marilyn Rodgers, is preparing for a new assignment. Not one to drop me unattended, Captain Rodgers asks if there is any physical therapist I prefer.

"No, who do you recommend?"

"Kyla is right for you," Captain Rodgers says. "She has worked with others who have suffered amputation of one leg below the knee and one above."

Kyla turns out to be the perfect choice.

Motivated more than ever by the people who welcomed me home, I push myself with back-to-back sessions, hoping to hasten the day I will be fit enough to stand up and walk out of here. It doesn't hurt my chances that Kyla, my PT angel, pushes me to the brink of endurance and pain, strengthening the core muscles in my mid-section, regenerating strength in my arms, hips, and stumps. Kyla works me hard but with incredible compassion, a great sense of humor, and precise knowledge of my limits.

My primary concentration is PT although I spend some time in occupational therapy, where they focus on the fine motor skills required to recover the more precise functions needed to grab small items with injured hands. They actually have set up a typical apartment in the OT department to work on all the little details in life that were once second nature. For me that means learning the best way to get in and out of the shower, how to fall, how to get in and out of the wheelchair, reach into cabinets, get in and out of bed, and find new ways to accomplish ordinary tasks.

In early June, Walt Fricke of the Veterans Airlift Command (VAC) invites us to lunch and says he has something we just have to see. He arrives in a shiny, blue Hummer H3 that was donated by General Motors to carry wounded soldiers to and from the airport. The Hummer is painted with a decorative U.S. flag and boasts a giant, brightly colored VAC logo, immediately converting the vehicle into a moving billboard to cruise the streets of Washington, D.C. Katie volunteers to be a driver. I take a couple missions as well and quickly discover I really enjoy driving it.

Walt's Hummer plants an idea. Now that we have escaped Ward 57 to the relative independence of Fisher House, it's time to test my wings and fly outside the base perimeter into "normal" civilization. Tee It Up for the Troops and RollX Vans gave us a van to use, but I need something of my own, something I can take home to Minnesota. Home! I like the sound of that, and I'm actually going to need a vehicle once I get there. It needs to be big enough for comfort with enough room for a whole family and a wheelchair, just in case I need to use the chair for a while. The Hummer is perfect; so, we buy one.

Although we've escaped from Walter Reed before, the trips take on a whole new feel in our own vehicle. We slip into nearby Silver Spring, Maryland, a fast-paced, upscale slice of the nation's capital. Silver Spring is concentrated, bustling, and alive with thousands of residents and daytime workers, intense traffic jams, massive pedestrian crowds, and canyons of office buildings and retail outlets.

As we venture out in public more and more, the experience is exhilarating and downright terrifying, all at the same time. People can't help but stare a bit, I probably would, too; but that takes some adjusting. Worse yet, the first few times out to eat, I panic. I can't explain it, but suddenly I just have to get out of there and back to my safety cocoon at Walter Reed. We can be waiting for our food, and I just can't take it another minute. I have to go, right now.

Katie has become a voracious reader to fill the long hours sitting by my side; so, Borders bookstore is a major focal point for our trips to town. For me the best part is heading off to Ruby Tuesdays for the Blondie dessert, about the only thing I really crave at the moment. Mostly, just getting out on our own, tasting the air of freedom, mingling with normal people, shopping, eating, and doing mundane tasks, is exhilarating.

It doesn't take long before I want more. Thinking back I remember that U.S. Senator Norm Coleman offered me a job in his Washington, D.C., office. I wonder if the offer was real. One phone call and I'm hired as an intern in the Hart Senate Office Building. My days start early at the hospital with two PT sessions back to back, a quick clean up, change into the standard D.C. uniform— suit and tie, and the commute to Capitol Hill. The job mostly involves reading constituent correspondence and offering assistance on matters involving the military, a frequent issue with 3,800 Minnesota Guard members in Iraq, not to mention other military members spread around the world.

When I'm not at the hospital or helping Senator Coleman, Katie and I play golf. We started in late March when Olney Golf Park offered free lessons to wounded warriors. They let us hit unlimited balls on the range, and their pros offered plenty of tips and free lessons. Not one to watch, Katie joined in. Katie was a star ice hockey player in high school, and her athletic skills were evident immediately.

When my prosthetics specialist, Tom O'Doherty, learns of my interest in golf, he quickly customizes my C-Leg. If I put my weight on my left toes and bounce three times, the C-Leg computer beeps, vibrates, and shifts into golf mode. In this mode the knee bends only slightly, enabling me to bend without having to worry about the knee buckling when I swing. Next he adjusts my left heel so that it turns slightly when I pivot. As amazing as my new legs are, I can't help but think how miraculous the human body is with all of the micro-movements we take for granted from every part of our body.

I put in a couple weeks on the driving range, taking lessons until I can't wait to get on an actual golf course. Announcing that golf provides the perfect mix of business with pleasure, Tom hauls me to Sligo Creek Golf Course, another place where they are very supportive of wounded warriors. It only takes one taste of playing golf again and I'm hooked. Katie and I start playing nine holes every other day. Golf proves to be the perfect training exercise for my balance. It's a big turning point where I begin walking much more, leaving the wheelchair behind. Playing golf is an enormous confidence booster.

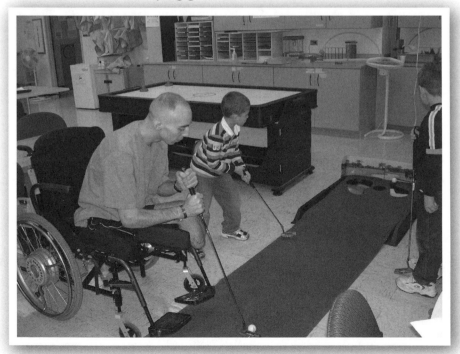

Brody and Elijah give me some tips before I head out to golf

**It's fantastic PT and mental adjustment getting out at
Sligo Creek Golf Course**

Buoyed with enthusiasm, Tom and I decide to try one of the area's premier golf courses. We jump in the Hummer and head off to Blue Mash Country Club not far from Walter Reed. The strange name comes from the colloquial pronunciation of marsh. The terrain is a blue-tinged clay soil dotted with lush marshes inspiring the name Blue Marsh in the area where freed slaves settled during the Civil War.

We sign in, pay our fees, and receive a blue flag, the nationally accepted designation for a disabled player that enables me to ride the golf cart right up to the edge of the greens. Approaching the first green, we're lost in the natural beauty of the course when a shrill noise shatters the moment and the course manager charges up behind us.

"You're probably going to struggle out there today," he says.

"No, we're good," I smile and prepare to putt.

"Are you sure you're going to be fine? It's pretty hot. I can give you a rain check."

"We're good." This is getting annoying.

"I don't want you driving on the fairways at all."

"What am I supposed to do?" I respond, growing more puzzled by this guy.

"You're going to have to walk up there."

"Okay, I'll drive in the rough and get as close as I can."

Still uncertain what is bothering him, I carefully maneuver the cart through the rough and drive as close to the third green as possible without leaving the rough.

"I thought I told you..." his voice erupts behind us just as Tom, an extremely quiet, mild-mannered guy, is about to putt.

"Okay," Tom slams his putter to the ground. "I have been really patient with you, but you're starting to piss me off! You're being a real jerk. We're out here just having a round of golf, and I got a wounded soldier trying to do his physical therapy. Just leave us alone."

Tom turns and prepares to putt as the course manager mumbles something my way.

"Excuse me?" I say.

"I told you this and you don't listen."

"I listened and I'm trying to do what you want. Your people gave me the blue flag. If I'm not welcome on your course just be man enough to tell me I'm not welcome."

"I could kick you off. You're lucky to have that blue flag."

"LUCKY TO HAVE THIS BLUE FLAG? YOU CALL THIS LUCKY?" I rip the stinking blue flag off the cart and whip it over his head into the woods. "Lucky to have the blue flag? Fuck you, asshole!"

"It's time for you to leave," he glares at me.

We don't need his sendoff; we're already heading for the clubhouse when three guys who were playing on the next hole come up and ask what the problem is.

"You guys should get a free round of golf," they assert, adding that they are members and will see that the incident is reported. They apologize.

Tom storms into the clubhouse, points out the conditions for a blue flag as described in the official golf rules book, and demands a full refund while I try to calm down at the parking lot. We get our refund.

After that Tom and I hit the links about once a week, but never again at Blue Mash and never another problem anywhere over the blue flag.

Golf is great therapy, mental and physical, and Tom always brings along his tools to make adjustments in my prosthetic legs. I continue playing golf several times a week, usually with Katie, who generally beats me and always complains when she doesn't hit par.

Chapter 38

THE WHITE HOUSE, AT LAST

I'm getting closer and closer to heading home, and that just pushes me to work harder every day in PT. But one major goal is yet to be accomplished—The White House visit.

I have met President Bush twice: shortly after I arrived when I received the Purple Heart, and again in the PT room where we talked at length. But neither of those were "the" visit. Over the months, everyone on Ward 57 knows about my desire to meet the president; so, whenever someone plans a trip to Pennsylvania Avenue, the nurses and therapists quickly add, "Don't forget Kriesel." So, when the Red Cross pulls together a group of wounded warriors for the big trip across town, it's not surprising to hear my name called. Katie and I pile into the bus with several other families.

Special thrills start immediately on arrival as we enter a classic, old wooden elevator that normally is reserved only for the president, and we slowly, very slowly, rise to the West Wing for a grand tour of the Blue Room and offices, and a peek into the Oval Office. While I pose for a photo in the archway to the Oval Office, Katie slips into the reception area and samples the fragrance of a bouquet of fresh roses. Sometimes you need to stop and smell the roses, especially in the White House.

The procession moves to the Rose Garden, then into a large reception area where the president frequently hosts foreign dignitaries and other special guests, such as wounded warriors.

Photographers record the moment for history before the president orders everyone but the wounded and their families to leave. He turns to us and says, "I'm sorry you had to go through this. We are very proud of you and what you have overcome; what you have sacrificed for this country. I want you to know that I would never put you in harm's way and would not continue to put men and women in harm's way if it were not absolutely necessary for our national security. I had to make this decision, and it was the right decision. Keep up the good work. Get better and go back to your families."

We feel his sincerity and sense his pain in having taken responsibility for our injuries.

He moves into the crowd and takes time to look in the eyes and talk directly with every soldier. One young woman who lost both legs just below her knees was just beginning to walk. President Bush invites her to walk across the room on his arm. It's very personal with each soldier as he makes his way around the room.

He's talking to a guy next to Katie and me when he suddenly recognizes us from Walter Reed. "Hey there, guys." He spins and wraps an arm around me.

Katie and I chat with President Bush in
the White House

Katie stops to smell the roses in the White House

Welcoming Eng Yang home from Iraq

Chapter 39

THE HOMECOMING

July 19, 2007

I'm not quite ready to leave Walter Reed, but there is no way I am going to be sitting in Washington, D.C., when my unit comes home. Dr. Brad Zagol removes my colostomy, hooks up my colon, and sends me off to homecoming at Fort McCoy, Wisconsin, a large Army base 160 miles east of St. Paul down I-94. It's where returning troops are debriefed, examined, and counseled, usually for a week before going home to their families.

Walter Fricke and his Veterans Airlift Command (VAC) steps up once more and offers to fly us home. We have lunch to discuss it. I suggest moving his VAC Hummer back to Minnesota where it will be a moving billboard for fund-raising, and we offer to drive it home rather than take another flight back. Walt agrees.

In Vietnam, Walt was a helicopter pilot who was wounded on a mission in October 1968 near the Cambodian border when a rocket misfired, exploding in the cockpit, launching shrapnel into Fricke's thigh, severing his left foot at the ankle. Although doctors prepared to amputate his foot, he fought them off and eventually recovered. A bigger challenge for Fricke than his injuries was making contact with his fiancée and parents, a problem that grew even worse once he landed at Fort Knox, Kentucky, and realized they could not afford to travel from Michigan to be with him over the Thanksgiving week. The mental trauma Fricke endured during those weeks alone in an Army hospital ultimately gave birth to Veterans Airlift Command.

After recovering from his war wounds Walt worked briefly as a cropduster, then an investment banker in Minneapolis. He built his own investment banking company that focused on the mortgage business and became very successful.

Recognizing storm clouds on the economic horizon, the cunning pilot sounded the alarm early on; but his voice was drowned out by the dark clouds of greed. He started an organization to address the coming tsunami of foreclosures, which was deployed successfully and still operates on a national basis, but he found few allies in a system where every self-indulged player expected to get rich and pull out before the coming crash. Just like a falling airplane, there's no safe way to bail out once you drop too close to the ground.

In 2006 Walt fielded a call from the Department of Defense in search of someone to fly a wounded Marine from Melbourne, Florida, home to Camp Lejeune in North Carolina, igniting a flood of memories. Walt couldn't do the flight himself, but he found a buddy in Florida who owned a plane and asked him if he could do a "hero flight."

The friend said, "Absolutely" and volunteered to pitch in anytime. The idea was planted and, over the next three years, it germinated into the Veterans Airlift Command, a nonprofit organization using more than 1,500 private pilots.

The VAC office technically is located in St. Louis Park, Minnesota, and is staffed by Fricke and his daughter; but actually it resides in a cell phone lodged in Fricke's pocket. It's a phone that rings day and night wherever Fricke happens to be. He quickly launches into operation, sending out the word that he needs a pilot. Within minutes he has multiple replies from those volunteering to haul heroes and their families free of charge and free of red tape.

Back at Walter Reed, confirmation comes that my brothers in Bravo Company are heading home at last after a record-long deployment of twenty-two months, including the six months training in Mississippi and sixteen months in Iraq. Bravo Company served the longest deployment in combat of any military unit since World War II. Another Minnesota Red Bull unit served seventeen months in WWII.

Minnesota's National Guard left their blood throughout Europe and North Africa during that WWII deployment. The Red Bulls were the first American Division deployed to Europe in January 1942 and in North Africa the 34th Infantry Division fired the first American shells against Nazi forces.

Minnesota's National Guard traces its history to 1850, six years before statehood, when Guard units protected early settlers and provided the only line of defense during the Dakota (Sioux) Indian War of 1862. They were the first unit to volunteer for the Civil War and distinguished their unit with a gallant charge at Gettysburg on July 2, 1863, where only forty seven of 262 soldiers survived. They held the Union position at Cemetery Ridge, stopping Confederate troops, and served in the Civil War battles at Bull Run and Antietam.

During the sixteen-month deployment to Iraq, Bravo Company searched more than 331,500 vehicles and 15,000 local citizens at Camp Fallujah, discovered 1,500 IEDs before they exploded, drove more than 2.2 million convoy miles, completed 107 reconstruction projects worth $11 million dollars, built or upgraded seven water purifications plants, constructed ninety miles of roads, and provided training for an Iraqi battalion in Al Anbar Province.

For me, waiting for my Army brothers to return, while I was recuperating at Walter Reed for eight months, felt like a lifetime. That all evaporates the instant they roll off their civilian charter aircraft at Volk Field, a military air base ten minutes from Fort McCoy. One by one they engulf me in enthusiastic brotherly hugs.

I spot Tim Nelson, who was doing his best to keep me motivated at the blast site the last time I saw him. Nelly jumps to the head of the line, bull-rushes me, and gives me a crushing hug.

"Great to see you, man," he says. "You look good. You look really good." He opens the vice grip of his big arms, grabbing both shoulders, and pushes me out at arm's length to examine me like he was shopping for a new suit.

"Better than last time?" I ask.

"A lot better!"

"I heard you yelling, man, and I wasn't going to let go if you were telling me not to."

Todd Everson is the next guy trying to squeeze the wind out of me. "You saved my ass! I would be dead without you." Todd was one of the guys who jumped from the Bradley to apply my tourniquets and tend to my wounds. Everson, Gallant and Seed truly were my first responders—the guys who kept me from dying in the desert.

Duty interrupts momentarily as Tim and the guys file over to the hanger to turn in their weapons. Then everybody starts talking at once. It's nearly impossible to understand a word that's being said, but, somehow, that doesn't matter. The guys have another week to go before they can head back to Minnesota for their personal reunions, but for the moment it is an intense hanger celebration in the shadow of prominent photographic memories of Bryan McDonough, Corey Rystad, and Jimmy Wosika on giant display boards. Amid the joy of coming home, the images of three brothers temper the mood. Every soldier absorbs the sobering reality that Bryan, Corey, and Jimmy didn't make it home.

War stories, handshakes, and hugs carry on for nearly an hour before the commander announces that it's time to head to the barracks for clean up and a mass move to McCoy's, the MWR Center at Camp McCoy. I drop Katie and the boys at our hotel to get ready while I head for McCoy's.

On the short route to McCoy's I spot a Marine walking that direction. What are the Marines doing here? Then I realize it's Marine Sergeant Major Walter O'Connell, Colonel George Bristol's top NCO from Camp Fallujah, with (my) First Sergeant Elwood.

"You guys need a ride?" I ask, easing alongside the veteran warriors.

McConnell breaks into a mammoth grin and spits out in his distinctive Boston Irish brogue, "Yes, I'm not too fricken proud to take a ride from Sergeant Kriesel."

He hops in, and we laugh all the way to McCoy's where Colonel Bristol is already mingling with the troops, handing out his personalized coins, patting every back, and telling every single guy how much he respects what they did. He explains that he cannot attend tomorrow's formal ceremonies because he and McConnell are flying back to Camp Pendelton first thing in the morning for a new deployment; so, he needs to meet and greet everyone tonight.

All the medals in the world could not do as much for me as having one of the top commanders from the U.S. Marine Corps and his senior sergeant show up to welcome home a company of National Guard soldiers. Two brilliant Marines who have served several tours of duty in combat are taking time to salute us Minnesota grunts. That is huge for me and every guy I know.

After shaking as many hands as possible, I run back to the hotel to bring Katie and the boys to the party.

I grab a bucket of beer and mingle with the enormous crowd and run into my cousin, Ricky Kriesel. He was part of the reason I re-enlisted and I want to spend some time with him, but it's just not possible with hundreds of guys milling about like bees in the hive. My sons try a little bowling, and once again they are the center of attention for my company of brothers—their uncles. It's incredible watching these two little guys mixing it up with a bunch of real-life heroes, something they will remember forever.

McCoy's is a massive place for the troops, with bar and lounge, game rooms, bowling alley, and more. The celebration provides a perfect opportunity for Katie to actually meet Everson, Gallant, and many of the guys who she has heard about so often that introductions aren't necessary. Fortunately, McDonough, Rystad, and Wosika were among the guys she and my boys had met before we deployed to Iraq.

Following a short night, Bravo Company spills out of the Fort McCoy barracks and falls into formation. First Sergeant Elwood barks out orders, and the troops snap to attention. It's almost a private performance as Katie and I and the boys, the only family on post, grab folding chairs to relax in the shade and enjoy the formation. Suddenly everybody in the second rank except Tim Nelson moves in perfect unison one pace to the left exposing an open spot between Sergeants Nelson and Jay Horn—my spot as Alpha Team Leader. The entire platoon turns our way, waves to me, and points to my spot.

Totally surprised, I get to my feet and eagerly move toward them with emotions coursing through my body. Given my emotions at the moment, it would be difficult making the short trip on two good legs, but I manage to slide into formation. The first sergeant barks out names of award recipients, and I hear my name. Moving forward, I proudly accept my Combat Infantry Badge and stand tall as LTC Gregg Parks approaches and pins the Bronze Star Medal on my chest. It is one of the coolest moments of my life, not because of the medal, but because I realize that I am still one of them and, no matter what, I always will be.

I'm back in the Barbarians Brotherhood at Fort McCoy

LTC Gregg Parks pins the Bronze Star Medal on my chest

Chapter 40

DISCOVERING WHAT LIFE
IS ALL ABOUT

The party's over in a blink, and we head back to Walter Reed. The celebration pumped me up more than a case of energy drinks. Now I'm even more determined to clear the deck and get home to Minnesota.

My permanent prosthetics are ready. They feel great, and I'm ready to get on with life. We spend a couple weeks completing paperwork, running the gauntlet of medical inspections, and saying our good-byes.

As we're packing for the trip home, I remember talking to Chris Hawkey of KFAN sports radio when I was at the station in May; he had mentioned that they would like to have me on the show when I come home for good. A quick call to Hawkey and I'm set for a week of daily visits on the *Power Trip Morning Show*. I have a blast, and the people at the station must enjoy having me around because they ask me to come in every Tuesday. They also set up a regular weekly gig dubbed "In the Kries" on Thursdays when I head out to the Minnesota Vikings training field at Winter Park (in the western suburb of Eden Prairie) for interviews.

The Vikings interviews are always a bit of a challenge that demand my very best ad lib effort because I never know in advance who will be the subject of the day. Assistant Director of Public Relations Tom West, a guy with the build of a middle linebacker, meets me and arranges a different interview each week with a special teams' player, defensive coordinator Leslie Fraser, rookie running back Adrian Peterson, or anybody connected with the team. West is the Vikings main PR guy, the unidentified man in a nice suit you see every Sunday on television, shadowing quarterback Brett Favre anytime Favre isn't in the game.

The first few months back in Minnesota blow by in a blur of activity with frequent news media interviews, public appearances, doctor and VA hospital appointments, visits with every person I ever met and many new friends, and daily trips to the site of our new house. It's exhilarating and exhausting all in one.

In the midst of my frenetic pace, Will Bernhjelm, a Guard buddy from Kosovo and Iraq, calls to suggest that I need a break from the grind. We make plans for a quick trip to Las Vegas to unwind with a little drinking and gambling.

We're literally packing when I realize the large bump on my lower back near where my busted spine and pelvis were fused is getting bigger and painful. Fearing a new round of infection, I manage to get a quick appointment with Dr. Bruce Bartie, an orthopedic surgeon in Stillwater. Within seconds Dr. Bartie confirms my infection fears and says he needs to cut my back open to remove the screws from my pelvis and spine.

"No way," I react in shock and fear as I get up and walk out. "I need to talk to Dr. Potter."

Staggering out to my car, I don't know whether to scream or break down and cry, but I manage to email Potter at Walter Reed, "I need to get hold of you right away." Hardly a minute passes before my phone rings.

"John, calm down and tell me what is wrong." Potter eases my fear immediately.

I lay out the story. "There's got to be another way."

"Nope. He's right. They need to remove those screws and eliminate the infection. I'll get the files to him, right now. John, I know it sucks, but you're going to be just fine; and the good news is they should not have to replace those screws."

Reluctantly, I return to Dr. Bartie's office and make plans for the surgery. The only bright spot, he says I can go to Las Vegas and do the surgery when I return.

Las Vegas has always been my favorite place to visit. I have made an annual visit there every year since turning twenty-one, except when I was out of the country. But now I worry that somehow, being hurt, it won't be as much fun. For Will it is his first visit. We gamble, drink, gamble, and drink some more. The only downside is coming back Monday night and getting ready for surgery the next morning.

Surgery goes as smoothly as something like that can go, and I get back to learning about life after a short recovery. I'm still recovering at Lakeview Hospital in Stillwater when Bryan Harper, senior marketing manager for the Vikings, calls to ask if I can attend the December 2 game and blow the gigantic Viking horn that reverberates through the Metrodome at the start of each game, signaling the team to burst onto the field. When Harper discovers that December 2 is my Alive Day, he gives me tickets to invite one hundred buddies to the game. At first I'm thinking it's going to be difficult giving out a hundred tickets—that thought survives about an hour when all the tickets are gone.

Alive Day is a soldier's celebration of the day he didn't die, and mine is December 2. We stage a tailgate party and rock the Dome only two days after I escape from the hospital after back surgery. The Vikings do their part by dismantling the Detroit Lions 42–10 with rookie running back Adrian Peterson running over would-be tacklers for 116 yards and two touchdowns. Minnesota quarterback Tarvaris Jackson adds touchdown tosses to Bobby Wade and Sidney

Rice, and Aundrae Allison enters the record books with a 103-yard kickoff return to seal the romp.

As if the game wasn't enough, Brad Madsen, director of community relations, calls to invite me to the Vikings practice field, explaining that each week Coach Brad Childress hosts a special guest family. The private tour is made extra special when I learn that we'll be going to the Saturday, December 29, walk-through before the team heads to Denver for a Sunday game. These practices generally are closed–door affairs to avoid the risk of enemy team espionage.

On Saturday, Katie, Elijah, Brody, and I climb into our truck with unbridled excitement and head west across I-494. Arriving at the Vikings practice headquarters, we meet Madsen, who gives us the grand tour including prime photo opportunities with the boys sitting at owner Zygi Wilf's desk and standing at the team lectern where Coach Childress holds his press conferences. Coach Childress greets us warmly on the indoor practice field where he brings together the whole team and tells my story. Players express sincere enthusiasm in their greetings, and it gives me a chill to think that these guys with household names are applauding me.

After the game, Coach Childress encourages me to watch Sunday's game with an eye for the plays the team worked on during the walk-through. The inside knowledge makes that game very special; particularly when I recognize what is coming and the play works to perfection—no wonder they don't want potential spies attending the Saturday practice. Unfortunately, not enough of the plays work to perfection as the Vikings miss a chance at the play-offs by losing 22–19 and finish the season 8–8.

A downside to my back surgery is the wound VAC, a sort of vacuum cleaner for infection that is attached to my back. Other than getting in the way a bit when I sit, it emits a strange noise every five or ten minutes when it activates, creating a sound like a fart coming from my lower back. It's particularly embarrassing when I return to classes at Brown College in Minneapolis, a school that specializes in teaching radio skills.

DISCOVERING WHAT LIFE IS ALL ABOUT

"Oops, that's me again," I apologize to class the first few times. Subdued snickers and smiles evaporate once people know what is making the noise. My back VAC functions well, except for the embarrassing noise during recordings and on-air sessions—difficult explaining that sound on the air.

My fart machine isn't a major problem, but I quickly realize this school is not helping me. I am learning more from my volunteer gig at KFAN than at school. It doesn't make sense sitting in school when I could be home with my boys instead of attending meaningless classes. I've already spent way too much time away from my family. I'm not going to miss another minute with the boys. The process also convinces me that radio is not my thing. I love my volunteer work on KFAN, but it probably isn't going to be as much fun if it becomes a real job.

What *is* a problem after surgery is the need to clean out infection every few days. A nurse comes to the house and removes the tiny sponges, which always manage to start adhering, and cleans the wound. It hurts like hell, but over time the wound starts to heal and we beat back the infection.

Just in time for the holidays, we move into our new house in Cottage Grove and use the winter to settle into our new normal routine. When spring expels the snow and cold weather from Minnesota, our neighbors (who have been merely shadows sliding silently past windows all winter) come out to play and we jump in. Well, at least I roll in on my golf cart. I love driving around the neighborhood, sharing a beer, or joining in a bonfire with my neighbors, my new friends. It's a fantastic neighborhood and a day never goes by that I don't look around my house and say, "Wow, this really is my house, my neighborhood."

Cost of construction is less than anticipated because Bill and Ron's (Derrick Custom Homes) sub-contractors donated much of their time and materials. Even Great Plains Millwork provided the windows. I don't even know what that saved us, but I do know these are the very best windows available; we are definitely appreciative.

While the house is under construction, we squeeze into a tiny, two-bedroom apartment in Woodbury, and I make a point to visit the construction site every day, spending time with the workers, showing how much we admire their work, and expressing our thanks. It is the least I can do. Watching my house rise out of a hole in the earth is amazing. The boys still have their little blue hard hats.

December is pure chaos, pleasant chaos, with the move, Christmas, and housewarming but definitely a mental meltdown. Knowing how much I have grown to love poker, Katie gives me a trip to the World Series of Poker Academy at Caesar's Palace in Indiana, just across the Ohio River from Louisville, Kentucky. I'm looking forward to spring when I can head there.

Chapter 41

BLISS TURNS TO TENSION

As my world seems to improve on one front, problems boil to the surface at home. While I am preoccupied with my struggle to get my head around who I am, that becomes a big problem for Katie. She has become very annoyed with me, and as any wise husband knows, it's best to let her explain it her way.

Katie speaks out:

Coming home, John just lost who he was. He was busy telling everyone he was fine and everything was great, but he was just lost as a person. He had to go out and do all these things to prove to everybody that he was fine. He'd get an idea and he'd hit it 180 miles an hour, such as, "I'm going to be on the radio every day." Then, "I'm going to school full-time and that needs to be my thing. Screw everybody else's schedule; I got to take care of me."

He was having trouble realizing that he needed to be around his family. But he thought it was a good time to go catch up with every friend he had ever had, play golf, and have a blast every day.

There was a lot of tension between us, but what it boiled down to was he just didn't know who he was anymore. That caught me off guard. When something like this happens, you're different. You are never going to be who you used to be. It doesn't mean you're better or worse, it just means you're different. Now you need to find out who you are again. It takes trying a bunch of different things, what works and what doesn't, what you like and don't like.

I wish someone had given me some warning that he was going to do that. I had spent so much time holding things together. I expected him to have his life together once we got home. But, instead he went crazy and there was great tension. Looking back I totally understand it, but living through it, I was like, *What are you doing?*

In the end, it's how people deal with any major trauma. It either brings you closer or you fall apart. We became more comfortable with our life. I used to feel that I could never say "no" to him. But I no longer need to do things for him. Even when he asks me do things for him, I say, "You can do that for yourself."

Maybe that sounds mean, but I know his limitations. I know if it's something he can't do. But if he's just being lazy, I call him out on it. Fortunately, there isn't much now that he can't do."

I no longer feel overwhelmed, and he doesn't feel like an invalid. He doesn't feel helpless or that I'm his mother. The counseling we had at Walter Reed and in Minnesota really helped, even if it did take us some time to understand it. We use what they told us. We had some tense moments, but we found our place. It just took time. Mostly, it was learning how to talk to each other all over again, how to say it's okay to be upset. It's okay to point out things that aren't correct, but to do it in a different way.

Chapter 42

BUILDING A NEW LIFE

January 2008

After the holidays, life gets quieter, much quieter. Deafeningly quiet. I don't know what to do. This is a whole new face of pain. At Walter Reed there was so much activity that I was always busy. It's easy to be positive and proud of your service when people are popping into your room every day just to say "thank you," but at some point you go home mentally as well as physically in search of something called normal.

The first few months back home were surreal with the constant activity of the new house, media interviews, public appearances, the holidays, and all of my medical adventures, but suddenly life has come to a screeching halt. There are no people down the hall who have lost their parts; Katie is at work, and I am alone. Well, not totally alone, I have the boys and there is nothing like hauling them off to school and picking them up, but most of the day I'm alone.

As adults we dwell on how much we must teach our little ones; amazingly, often we are doing the learning. My kids are teaching me so much it's incredible. To them I am just the same old dad, nothing's changed. I start thinking about bad things and a little voice interrupts, "Dad, let's go play catch." Okay, cool. That's it—I need to be Dad.

When I speak to groups or at schools, I always tell people to take inventory of what's good about life, appreciate the little things, slow down. Looking at Brody and Elijah, I realize it's time to take my own advice.

The Minnesota National Guard put together a mandatory Yellow Ribbon Program with thirty-, sixty-, and ninety-day group counseling sessions for all returning warriors. Obviously, they need to do something. They mean well, but it is of little value to me. It almost feels like they're saying, "We want you to get over the whole war thing in thirty, sixty, or ninety days." But it doesn't work that way. At that point people don't even know what their problems are. At thirty days I was just basking in the glow of making it back. The demons are obscured. But they lurk in the back of my mind just waiting to pounce when I least expect to see them. This takes more than ninety days.

It's like working with kids. I can tell them over and over what to do, share my knowledge and experience; but they don't get what I'm talking about until they discover it for themselves. It's the same with soldiers. I love getting together with the guys, talking about stuff, knowing they are there if I need someone, but in the end, I just have to fight through it and hope there is someone there who loves me enough to make it work. Mostly, it just takes time, *a lot* of time.

As 2008 unfolds I'm much improved physically and decide it's time to figure out where life is headed, take control. But, first things first. Katie gave me the trip to the World Series of Poker Academy at Caesar's Palace; so, I have to go. By the time we work out all the details and commitments it's April, and I'm on the road to Indiana all by myself. That's when it hits me: this is my very first solo trip since the explosion. I am totally alone and it's incredibly liberating. I really don't need or want anyone to carry things, move my wheelchair, care for me—I can do it myself.

After signing in at the WSOP Academy I head down to a sports bar in the hotel just to relax and get my head ready for poker. I don't know a soul here but quickly make friends with some of the other Academy candidates when my cell phone goes off. The number isn't familiar, but a little voice deep in my head tells me to answer.

"Hey, John, how ya doing?" the familiar voice of State Command Sergeant Major Edward (Scott) Mills comes through. Mills is a great sergeant major, always checking with his guys to ensure we are being well taken care of. Anytime I see him he says, "Hey, John, are they giving you everything you need? You tell me if they're not." For a lot of people that's just hollow words, but Sergeant Major Mills means what he says.

"John, we want you to come to the Governor's Fishing Opener next month with a few other soldiers as honored guests."

"Wow, that's fantastic. I'll be there."

I'm barely back from Indiana, and it's time for the biggest annual holiday in Minnesota, the opening day of fishing at Breezy Point Resort in Pequot Lakes. With a population slightly more than five million, Minnesota issues in excess of two million fishing licenses. It always appears that every one of those licenses is in use in early May when the season launches. Lakes are so filled with boats that you can almost walk across most of them without getting wet feet. The only problem arises when Mother's Day coincides with the opener, a true formula for family crisis. Fortunately, there's no conflict this year.

Since 1948 Minnesota governors have launched every fishing season, lending publicity to an enormous industry that generates $5 billion annually for the state's economy on 15,291 lakes, 6,564 rivers and streams, and Lake Superior. One of those many rivers is the mighty Mississippi that originates in Minnesota near Lake Itasca, tumbling 2,320 miles south through ten states before dumping into the Gulf of Mexico ninety miles south of New Orleans.

Breezy Point is a classic Minnesota northwoods escape that has hosted outdoorsmen and families for decades, even a few Chicago gangsters in the 1920s and '30s. Arriving Friday night before the big opener, I check into my room and head down to the main lodge. The local VFW has invited Command Sergeant Major Corey Stigen, Lieutenant Colonel Jacob Kulzer, me, and several other injured soldiers over for drinks. Laughs and stories about wars recent and past fill the room. We share great moments with this pack of old warriors, screaming with laughter after every story. The stories get more bizarre as the night progresses.

Finally, we migrate back to Breezy Point and assemble in the new lounge area that features a large bar, swimming pool, and numerous games all set off by a rustic décor of natural wood, giant wildlife paintings, stuffed trophy fish, mounted wild animals, and historic local photographs. We're carrying on the party when I recognize three guys at the next table—Minnesota Vikings players Jim Kleinssaser and Steve Hutchinson, two of the largest human beings on the planet, and PR-man Tom West. West slides over and greets all my guys.

Lieutenant Colonel Kulzer sits down next to me and says, "You should come to work for me." Here's another offer, and once again I'm not certain what it means or if it's real.

"I mean it," he reads my mind. "We got a spot for you."

Next morning we're up at four-thirty a.m., incredibly early considering that we were in the lounge until two a.m. I'm suffering a nasty hangover and quickly realize that sitting in a boat in the early morning darkness during a miserable, cold rain is no great hangover cure. Worst of all, I don't catch a thing, not even a cold. But laughter and good times return when we decide it's just too damn miserable to fish—let's go eat the shore lunch, that's walleye, Minnesota's prize fish. After lunch I decide enough is enough. My leg is aching, and I shouldn't be getting it wet, it would be a disaster to have a computer meltdown up here in the Northwoods.

Dinner is a formal program headed by Governor Tim Pawlenty, who did better than me fishing by catching a couple of small walleyes. His wife, Mary, a judge, outdid us both. The program is already underway when Lieutenant Colonel Kulzer tells us he needs a couple soldiers to speak. I've been doing more than my share of public speaking lately and decide to leave the talking to the other guys. The colonel goes first, then he leans my way and says, "Kriesel, you're next."

After all the drinking and yelling last night, my voice is barely a whisper. I can hardly make noise, let alone speak, but the colonel insists. The governor is already telling his favorite Kriesel story about how I said I was going to come back and take his job.

"I want to thank everyone for all the drink coupons last night," I eke out in a raspy voice putting a hand to my throat. "This is your fault." That gets big laughs; so, I launch into my best Iraq jokes and finish, telling them, "Minnesota is a great state. It was my great honor to serve it."

Lieutenant Colonel Kulzer greets me at the table with a broad smile and vigorous handshake. "That was a heck of a good speech, Kriesel. We'll talk soon about you coming to work for me."

All the way home I toss the idea around in my head. Sure, it's very flattering to be wanted, but is it a good idea? Financially there doesn't appear to be any benefit for me to stay in the Army and work when I can stay home and make the same money without the need for childcare. But, I can't stand just sit around doing nothing either, sitting home alone.

For days I can't get it off my mind. Then a thought erupts, and I call the lieutenant colonel. "If I retire from the Guard is there any way to get a civilian job working for you?"

"Yes, I think we can do that."

That's all I need, although the retirement process takes a bit longer than anticipated. On November 14, 2008, Katie and I travel to Fort Knox, Kentucky, and officially retire from the Army. It's even more emotional than I anticipated. I'm ecstatic that the long, drawn-out medical board process is over and eager to get on with my new job, my new life. Finally, I don't need to call my platoon sergeant every day to check in at CBHCO, the Community Based Health Care Organization. CBHCO is the Army's outpatient arm that permits active duty soldiers to obtain care at home that is coordinated with Walter Reed.

A twinge of sadness creeps in as I realize my military career is over. This is not the way I wanted it to end. I loved my job in the Army. Absolute finality hits when I sign the paper and someone hands me a DD214 (certificate of release from active duty), a small "retired U.S. Army" sticker and pin, U.S. flag, and a certificate of retirement along with a convenient cardboard box to haul everything away.

Outside it's a dreary, rainy day. It seems fitting. As I climb into our rental car, Katie asks, "Are you okay?"

I just nod and continue to absorb the reality of ending a ten-year career that covers all of my adult life. It's weird. This is no surprise—I made the choice and I have a new life planned that starts Monday with a new job, but that doesn't make it any less sad.

Driving off Fort Knox, we pass a large sign that says, "Buckle Up. Drive Safe. Thank You for Visiting Fort Knox." *Wow, this is it.*

I absolutely love the National Guard—it's people coming together from the same area, fighting for something they believe in, people who share the same beliefs, for the most part. We have excellent training, but what really matters is the brotherhood, a brotherhood of guys who want to help wherever they are needed, just do the right thing.

The following Monday morning, I report to the Minnesota National Guard office in Roseville to start a whole new career in the marketing department. I am responsible for creating advertisements, coordinating partnerships with Minnesota professional sports teams and local businesses, and educating the public on the mission and capabilities of the Minnesota National Guard.

Chapter 43

LOOKING DOWN FROM THE TOP OF THE MOUNTAIN

Fortunately, I never experienced the "why me" syndrome that hits many wounded warriors, but that doesn't mean my head doesn't hurt, or that I don't get angry. That happens, but not very often.

When I talk to students, I often say that before December 2, 2006, the worst day in my life was January 17, 1999, when Gary Anderson missed a field goal late in the fourth quarter, and the Vikings wasted a 15–1 season and a trip to the Super Bowl. Honestly, it's true. I thought that was a major tragedy, but the sun came up the next morning.

Waking up at Walter Reed and seeing that my legs were gone was devastating, but the sun came up and I was alive. It's tough, but there is no alternative except to move on. What made it work for me was the support system; a support system I didn't even know existed at first. Oh, I knew my wife and kids were there for me; but, when we came home and the whole community made us part of their family, I knew everything was going to work out.

Looking back at the constant psychological testing I endured at Walter Reed, I am still not certain whether all the questions and memory tests were designed to discover lingering brain damage or to help me deal with the psychological damage of losing my friends and two legs. In a strange way, the annoying, incessant questions about every minute detail of the explosion probably helped me deal with the aftermath better than some of the guys who returned without physical injuries and were thrown back into society with minimal counseling. I no longer have nightmares. It's not that I am not haunted by the savagery of battle; it's just that I realize that, although I cannot change the past, I can make the future better for my family. I firmly believe that Bryan, Corey, Jimmy, and the rest of us sacrificed immensely to make the world a better place for everyone here and in Iraq.

When I was in the hospital, there were times when I was horrified and thought about the craziness of what happened to me. I almost couldn't believe my legs were blown off. It helped that I was dulled by constant medication, but the drugs didn't stop the dark thoughts from creeping in now and then. Strangely, it was just the fight to keep going that helped more than anything. I came to realize there was no room for sadness or emotions. This is my life now.

Katie describes our life at Walter Reed as an out-of-body experience, where it was almost as if we were watching ourselves on television. She confesses to me now that she went through some very sad times, especially when I suffered a setback; but she masked her fear and sadness from me.

When we moved to Fisher House, I dealt with my own demons, but I hardly noticed what happened to Katie. In my neurotic, panicked state of mind, I practically drove her over the hill. Luckily, she didn't split, but there were times when she locked herself in the bathroom. In the hospital she was always there, but she also knew that there were plenty of nurses keeping track of medications, treatments, and emergencies. Suddenly she was my sole caregiver and I was pretty demanding, she says, "very demanding."

She was at the hospital around the clock, and it was the difference maker for me. She did exercises right alongside me and took care of my every need. Katie was a ragamuffin for nine months, running around in sweatpants and T-shirts and never getting her hair cut—and, she still was the best looking gal at Walter Reed.

"I had to do it that way," Katie says now, "because I'm a control freak. Amid the utter chaos, I felt that if I could control a piece of it, things would be okay. As long as I was in charge of something, I was helping—I was going to make him better. It worked for us, although it is not surprising that the other wives focused on their own lives because that's what the hospital staff kept saying. Just like when you take off in an airplane and the flight attendant cautions that in case of an emergency you should take oxygen yourself before trying to help anyone else, at WRAMC they tell you if you don't take care of yourself you won't be able to help him.

"But in the end that can build resentment," she recalls. "I can't tell you how many couples we saw fighting with each other. One wife just couldn't deal with it so she just went home to work and did her own thing. Now, he harbors strong resentment and their marriage is in a shambles."

That's not to say we didn't have our moments of extreme tension. In frustration one night shortly after we moved into Fisher House, probably one of those times she escaped to the bathroom, I unloaded on Katie.

"You don't know what it's like to be me," I shouted. "You don't know what it's like to have your legs blown off and lose your friends."

"That's true," she came back. "And, you don't know what it's like to be me. You don't know what it's like to get a phone call in the middle of the night, pack up my shit in one suitcase, and be gone for nine months and still be expected to hold everything together, worry about the kids, my job, and getting the bills paid while taking care of you."

Tension hung in the air for a couple days, perhaps because I knew she was right as much as anything else. Then I would remember all the good things I had and how many people were worse off than me. As for the tension, try locking any two people up in a small room for nine months and see what happens, even without the challenge of pain, frequent surgeries, and fear of death.

We made it through all the tension at Walter Reed and through my re-entry period at home. Our relationship is stronger than ever. Sometimes I even wonder how we did it; but, as Katie says, "We just love each other. If there was any part of me that didn't love you, I would have walked away, because it was horrible, difficult, and overwhelming."

Mostly, we made it because we have each other and we are very positive, strong people. I may be the luckiest guy on earth to have someone like her. Now we are in cruise control. Life is as normal as it's ever going to be.

We realize that our little family is the most important thing in the world. My injuries created an incredibly surreal period for us. It's not that we weren't a family, but we were forced to live in different places and there was nothing normal about our lives. Now, we are just this little family unit, just the four of us, or as Katie says, "We're like this little pod." A very happy pod, doing all the things normal people take for granted, and we relish normal.

Entering 2010 it suddenly occurs to me just what my new normal is all about. Life most definitely is good. My body is put back together. I have the most outstanding wife and kids in the world, and I have a great job that I enjoy.

In Kosovo and Iraq I looked into the eyes and hearts of weary, betrayed citizens to discover what happens when government fails its people.

If I can't fight, I can serve. One thing I have learned is that when doors of opportunity get slammed in your face whether by a bomb blast in Iraq, auto accident at home, loss of your job, death of a loved one, or any personal tragedy, new doors are waiting for you to push them open. Sure, I wish my body was normal, but that isn't going to happen. Many new doors have been thrown open to me that never would have been there. I just need to use these opportunities to help my family and to find new ways to honor all those who did not come home. Once you put aside pain, sorrow, and grief, your future is what follows tragedy, a new day with new opportunities.

Chapter 44

MY HEROES

In some ways all of the pain and suffering Katie and I endured is more than offset by the overwhelming generosity and outpouring of good will from so many people. If I learned anything from this horrific experience it is that there are many, many more good people than bad in the world. That is why we fought in Iraq, to give the good people in that part of the world the opportunity to share in the good life we have here in America.

Three of my brothers lived and died for the belief that everyone deserves to share our freedoms. As their brother, it is my obligation to ensure that their lives were not lost in vain and that America continues to stand up for freedom anywhere others are enslaved, free and open communication is prohibited, education is denied, or religion is dictated. I live to honor Bryan, Corey, and Jimmy, and all of my brothers in service who gave their lives to win these basic human rights for people they did not know.

This chapter has been by far the most difficult, because no matter how many changes I make, I am not satisfied. I cannot find words to sufficiently express or accurately describe what Bryan, Corey, and

Jimmy meant to me—their friendship and work ethic, and all that they stood for.

SGT Bryan McDonough

Bryan was one of those guys who was born to be a soldier. He was so good at it he made everything look easy, much like a professional athlete will make the most incredible action appear simple, until you try to do it. We met on the firing range at Camp Shelby at the beginning of our deployment. I realized immediately that Bryan was a superb machine gunner and when one of my guys departed with a bad back I quickly requested Bryan as the replacement.

Once we were together, it was like we had always known one another, and we did grow up almost neighbors. I attended White Bear Lake High School, and he was at Roseville High School in the next suburb. We discovered that we even knew some of the same people growing up and wondered how often we had crossed paths before joining the Guard.

Being Bryan's team leader made being good friends awkward at times, especially when I handed out extra duty or he drew some undesirable detail. Tension would hang over us, and he would go silent; then there would be a knock on my door, and there was Bryan. "Want to go to chow?" We would walk to the chow hall, chat, and eat like nothing had happened.

He was such a good soldier that he was named Soldier of the Quarter for Bravo Company, and then Soldier of the Battalion in November 2006.

We can't bring Bryan back, but his boundless energy, contagious smile, and profound commitment to doing the right thing lives on through the annual gathering of soldiers, friends, and family at the Bryan McDonough American Heroes Charity Golf Tournament at Oak Glen Country Club in Stillwater, Minnesota. Proceeds from the Tournament are used to assist wounded Minnesota soldiers and their families.

The Third Annual American Heroes Tournament drew 253 golfers, including many of the guys we served with and a few celebrities, such as Minnesota Twins coaches Ron Gardenhire and Steve Little. The tournament has grown so large that it has morning and afternoon sessions of eighteen-hole scramble play with lunch and dinner programs that bring in even more people for the massive silent auction and dance.

I share one last good time with Bryan and Corey two hours before the blast.

Bryan's golf tournament is my favorite day of the year. It is a day that everybody from our unit takes off work and gets together to play golf, laugh, drink, and reminisce. It is the one day of the year that we all go back to 2005 when we were together and things were normal. Bryan, Corey, and Jimmy are not at the tournament in body, but we know they are there.

I am proud to have had the opportunity to serve with Bryan, but even more proud to have had him as my friend.

SGT Corey Rystad

Corey was another guy I got to know at Camp Shelby when he hopped into the bunk above me and quickly became a little brother to me. Coming from a small town in northern Minnesota, he was the kindest person I ever met.

Every soldier talks about what they are going to do when they go home. We all tossed around crazy ideas and laid out goals. Corey was going back to school to become an x-ray technician in a rural northern community. I constantly urged him to move to the Twin Cities, mostly because I wanted all my guys nearby when we went home so we could hang out together. But, as much as I loved the hustle and bustle of the big city, Corey wanted quiet and fresh country air.

At his funeral more than a thousand people including Minnesota Governor Tim Pawlenty, U.S. Senator Mark Dayton, Congressman Collin Peterson, and nearly the entire city of Red Lake Falls crowded in and around St. Joseph's Catholic Church on December 13, 2006. The sun broke out that day adding uncharacteristic warmth to a December day in the far North.

The town's businesses closed, and flags dropped to half-staff on every building while their young hero was laid to rest between two tall pine trees in snow-covered northern Minnesota—far from the scorching Iraq desert where he died. His death brought the war home to Minnesota's remote farm region. In response to many requests, the funeral was broadcast live to Thief River Falls, Baudette, Karlstad, and other small towns that hug the Canadian border.

Like most soldiers, Corey was a good athlete. He lettered in football and hockey at Lafayette High School in Red Lake Falls where he graduated in 2004. He loved golf, hunting, and helping younger hockey players by organizing referees for the local hockey program. I often think back to our time at Pensacola Beach when Corey let my sons bury him in the sand, and he was enjoying it and laughing more than they were. He would have made a great father.

SSG James Wosika Jr.

A Minnesota State champion wrestler and football player for Highland Park High School in St. Paul (Class of 2000), Wosika served with the Minnesota National Guard in Kosovo and Iraq. Following high school, he returned frequently to help coach young wrestlers.

After Jimmy died, fifteen friends and relatives, including his sister Nichole, her husband John Stafford, and James Wosika Sr.,

Jimmy gives me a free ride in Kosovo

asked Minneapolis tattoo artist Tommy Reif to put portraits of Jimmy on their bodies in homage to their hero. Reif had created a tattoo for Jimmy when he was on leave in August 2006.

That image of Jimmy's picture on my computer screen along with the story that he had been killed is burned into my brain—it is still hard to believe that he is gone. When I think back to when we were young, wide-eyed privates the memories conjure up happy thoughts. We always talked about what it would be like when we became leaders, what we would do, and how we would lead. Those talks seem so long ago, but Jimmy became a great leader. His men respected him and the things he taught them.

It is easy to sit in an Armory on drill weekend and talk about what we would do in combat and how we would lead, but it is another thing to actually go into battle in Iraq and do it. SSG James

Wosika Jr. put his life on the line for the men in his team, and he most likely saved their lives in the process. I could not be more proud of him for what he did and the example he set for the soldiers that follow in his footsteps.

A final thought...

My heart aches just thinking about my friends. I believe in what our unit accomplished in Iraq, and I believe my friends gave their lives defending a worthy cause.

Often I find myself looking back at December 2, 2006, and it always feels to me that there was a plan all along for us to hit that IED. We took more photographs the day before, and on December 2, than on any other day. We all slowed down to enjoy just talking, laughing, and working together. We enjoyed that day.

Memories of the day expose a range of emotions. It was the day that two of my best friends died and I nearly died, but it was also the last time we were all together and happy. I think about our foot patrol that morning and the conversations we had. It is those conversations that I miss the most. I long for the random questions Corey would ask. I miss the times I was on overnight guard shift at the pump house and Corey or Bryan climbed into the tower where we talked through the night about nothing and everything. It's still hard for me to believe we will never have those conversations again. I still talk to them sometimes when I'm alone, but they don't talk back.

All of my wounds have healed except the hole in my heart. That wound will never heal, and that's fine with me. As strange as it sounds, it was the loss of my friends and my legs that showed me how to live my life; it taught me to see everything in a new perspective. Disaster was a cruel way to learn this lesson, but I will not waste it. I see every day as a gift, truly the first day of the rest of my life, and I will make today the very best day.

I miss those guys, and I am committed to making them as proud of me as I am of them.

EPILOGUE

By Jim Kosmo

In June 2009, Walt Fricke and I accompanied John on his triumphant return to Walter Reed Army Medical Center in Washington, D.C. As we left our hotel, heading to the hospital, John froze in his tracks at the sight of flashing red lights and the scream of a blaring siren. We stood at attention as a big bus hauling wounded warriors to begin their recovery at Walter Reed rolled past, and we all recognized how far John had come.

Several times every week mammoth mobile hospitals capable of carrying sixteen litters and fourteen ambulatory patients collect combat-wounded warriors at Andrews Air Force Base in Maryland for the ride to Walter Reed, and the beginning of another long journey. The battle to repair busted bodies and brains goes on every minute at Walter Reed where the patient count continues to grow.

Kriesel fulfilled a dream as he walked through the halls of Walter Reed Army Medical Center, greeting the "friends and family" that saved his life—no wheelchair, no walker, no crutches, and no canes. Trailing along behind the now-retired soldier, Walt Fricke and I observed precisely what John meant by "friends and family," although at times we found it difficult to match his pace as he relished in his ability to stand up and roam the hospital corridors.

Talking about Katie and our boys with physical therapist Kyla Dunlavey

Even a visit turns into a half-hour PT training session

"John!" a shriek bolted across the Physical Therapy Center the instant he entered. "How are Brody and Elijah? Where's Katie?" Kyla Dunlavey peppered him with questions, not waiting for answers before engulfing him in a giant hug—not an easy task for the slender therapist. Kyla's beauty, infectious laugh, flowing dark wavy hair, and penetrating brown eyes belie John's description of her as a very tough task master. "She pushed me until it hurt, but that's why I'm walking today," he explained.

**Sharing my story and lessons learned with students
is something I do as often as possible**

It had been nearly two years since John left Walter Reed, but Kyla and just about every doctor, nurse, and therapist we met knew him as though they had talked yesterday. Repeatedly, animated conversations erupted about his sons and wife and, within seconds, they are pulling out baby pictures. Everywhere we saw wounded soldiers, and I wondered how many have come and gone over the years, and yet these caregivers appeared to know every intimate detail in the personal lives of every soldier. This was no normal visit to the doctor; this was clearly a reunion of fast friends and adopted family.

Through every crisis, John emerged still standing, smiling, and demonstrating by example how to live a positive, successful life. Now, he shares his formula with young people every chance he gets—that is a true hero, literally a walking manual on how to succeed.

Shortly after we finished writing the book, John became a candidate for the Minnesota legislature, and it occurred to me that nothing could demonstrate his absolute recovery more emphatically

**Telling wounded warriors and WRAMC staff about benefits of
Veterans Airlift Command**

than going door to door talking with neighbors in his town. "If I
can't fight, I can still serve," he said with a broad smile.

Very early in the process of writing John's story, I met with a
group of writers at The Loft Literary Center in Minneapolis and
shared a draft of the first few chapters, whereupon one woman said
that I needed to tone down the injuries. She explained that she was
a physician working in the emergency room of a nearby hospital and
that no one could have survived with the massive injuries I described.
I explained that the book was not fiction. But, her comment
reminded me of the need to use extreme caution in writing so that
your true meaning is clearly understood. That is not always an easy
task, but that is why a writer always seeks help from good editors
and proofreaders.

EPILOGUE

As John and I dug into the book project, my background as a journalist caused me to question how John could always be so positive. But, he never wavered, never cancelled a meeting, and never stopped smiling. He said that he no longer suffered from bad dreams or felt anger; well, except when the Vikings lost.

It all seemed somewhat unrealistic, a bit Pollyanna-ish to me, and to just about everyone I met; so, I pushed harder and harder as we got to know each other. Finally, John and Katie admitted to some very rough days, bouts of sadness, and challenges to their relationship. They fought through everything together and came out even stronger, more in love.

In the end, I would love to reveal John Kriesel's magic formula for staying positive in the face of every incredible obstacle. After hours upon hours of digging and observing, I discovered that the answer truly is quite simple. It is the same formula that Dr. Norman Vincent Peale prescribed in his 1952 book, *The Power of Positive Thinking*, when he demonstrated how a proper attitude could change lives and win success in all pursuits.

Even in the early chapters of *STILL STANDING* you will note that John was a carefree, optimistic guy, and he never changed, he merely called upon an inner spirit. I don't know if you can teach a positive attitude to people or if it comes naturally, but attitude is what wins the day against any and all challenges. A win is not being crowned champion; true victory comes with achieving your own realistic goals.

A friend told me recently that he once met a blind man and consoled the man for his impairment.

"Impairment? I can do things that you cannot do."

"Such as?"

"I read in the dark. I can smell, hear, and feel things that you will never notice."

After losing his legs, John Kriesel discovered, "The list of things I can do is long, but the list of those things I cannot do is very short." Focus on what you can do.

John may reject the label of hero, but he definitely is my hero—not because of his injuries; it takes no special talent to get blown up. What makes John Kriesel a true hero is how he faced one disaster after another without giving up hope.

**John shares his return to WRAMC with author
CPT Jim Kosmo and VAC founder Walt Fricke**

★ ★ ★

ACKNOWLEDGEMENTS

Over the past two years, John Kriesel and I have become great friends, and in the case of the written word, I often do complete his sentences even if he does occasionally zing me for misspelling Baghdad or Katie. Our collaboration to write this book was possible only because we came to realize that, in spite of our great difference in age (I have grandchildren his age), we often think alike. It has been an incredible privilege for me to be able to get to know John and Katie, to tell their inspiring story, and to have the opportunity to meet all of the remarkable people who are the Red Bulls.

John and I would dearly love to write a paragraph or two about every single person who contributed to this book by sharing their story, reading, editing, contributing ideas, and helping us get it right. But there are so many people to thank that it would be another book. The following is a partial list of those who helped us.

Milt "Beaver" Adams

Lillian Bowell

Eric Bowen

Rev. Amy Brucker

Anne Brucker

Marly Cornell

April Michelle Davis

Kyla Dunlavey

Lisa Ericksen

SGT Todd Everson

Sara Ferguson

Walt Fricke

SSG Justin "Goose" Geslin

Steve Helland

SSG Kelly Jones

MAJ Tim Kevan

Rev. Sandee Kosmo

Michelle Kosmo

Shelley Bowell Kosmo

Katie Kriesel

Nancy Matthews

Tom McDonough

James Monroe

SFC Rene Montero

SSG Tim Nelson

MSG Brian Newcomer

Tom O'Doherty

MAJ B. Kyle Potter, MD

Amy Cutler Quale

CPT Charles "Chip" Rankin

Teresa Shinn

SSG Jay Trombley

Jordan Wiklund

James Wosika Sr.

Minnesota National Guard Public Affairs

IRAQ MAP

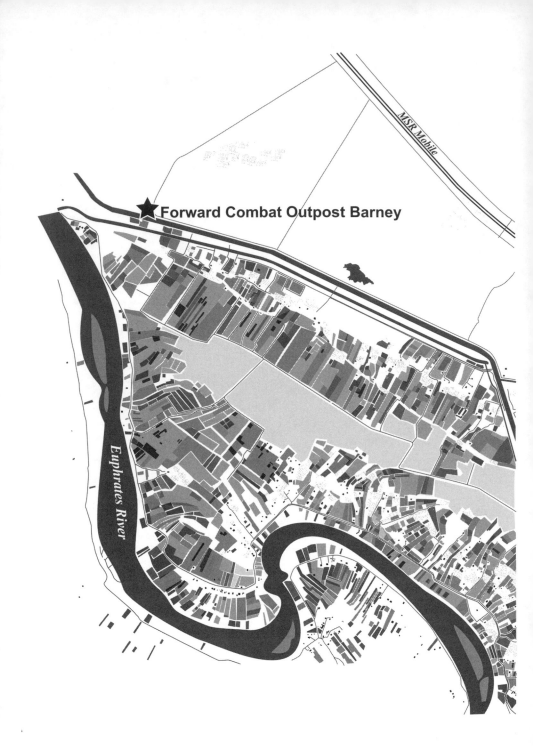

Forward Combat Outpost Barney

MSR Mobile

Euphrates River

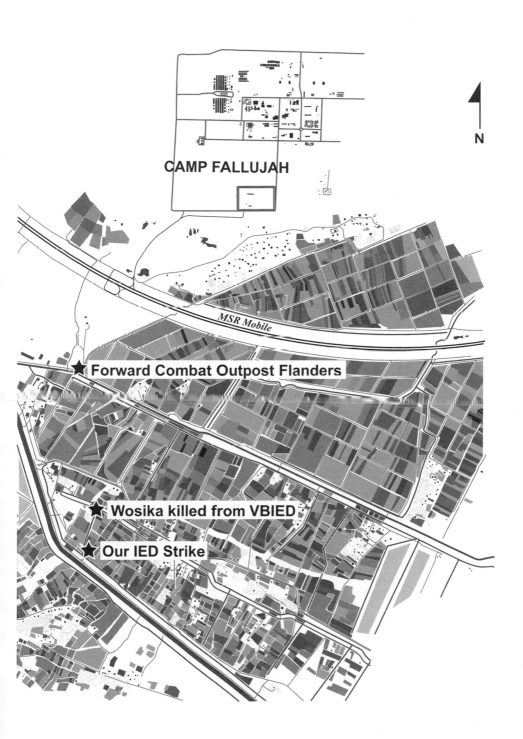

CAMP FALLUJAH

N

MSR Mobile

Forward Combat Outpost Flanders

Wosika killed from VBIED

Our IED Strike

ABOUT THE AUTHOR

Jim Kosmo is a national award-winning journalist, a licensed Mississippi riverboat pilot, and partner of Padelford Riverboat Company in St. Paul, Minnesota. He is a lifelong writer, having learned at the typewriter of his mother, Virginia, who was a correspondent for the St. Paul *Pioneer Press* in the 1950s. Before joining the family riverboat business, he was a newspaper editor and corporate public relations executive.

Captain Kosmo founded the Minnesota Valley Branch YMCA, served as chair of the Rivers Region of the national Passenger Vessel Association, served on the Bayport (MN) Planning Commission, and was elected a Bayport City Council member and mayor. Since 2008, he has served on the board of the St. Paul Rotary Club. He is a Paul Harris Fellow and Elmer L. Anderson Fellow. He also has created two endowed college scholarship funds.

Captain Kosmo balances his family life with eight adult children and ten grandchildren along with a successful career and the rewards of public service.

www.JimKosmo.com